About the time I had read (on holograms in Volume VII, I had a friend who was in a Care Center recovering from more heart surgery after having had his 5th heart attack in the last 20 years. He has additional health issues and is, to those of us who know him, a walking miracle. Understandably, his health issues have gotten his attention spiritually, and with each passing day over these many years, he was fully involved in listening to guided meditations, reading spiritual teachings and so on.

When I visited him on his birthday in the recovery center, already very limited by his weak heart, he was experiencing some depression following his surgery. His voice was on the weaker side and his energy was very low and, in fact, he expressed some disappointment that he had lived through the surgery. He is tired of living a very limited life which a weak heart brings.

Spirit moved me to talk to him regarding Jeshua's discussion about how we are and our life is a holographic projection of our consciousness and beliefs. If we want to change the hologram, we change our conscious projections. He listened intently and took a few moments to respond, and I could see this had gotten through to him, as his eyes widened and he responded rather quietly, "Yes, I like that; I really like that."

The next morning I called him to see how he was feeling, and when he picked up the phone, seeing my name on the call identifier, he answered with: "I AM in perfect health, I AM in full financial abundance and I AM the Universe listening to my declaration!" And I added, "You are the Universe responding to your declaration." He replied he liked that and would include that too. His whole countenance had changed, and he had a sparkle in his voice and was sounding more like his old self.

Now, of course, with all his spiritual studies, he had been practicing declarations for many years but this time it was different because it was coming enthusiastically from his heart as a result of this meaningful wisdom from Jeshua. Truly his beliefs had changed. He knew it and so did I. He is home now recovering once again and has made a remarkable recovery.

-- *Charlotte Walter*

ABSOLUTE LOVE, INFINITE LIGHT

Messages from Jeshua ben Joseph (Jesus)

Jeshua
The Personal Christ
Volume VII

Judith Coates

ISBN: 1878555170
ISBN 13: 9781878555175

Published by
Oakbridge University Press
Graphic design: Thomas Coates;
Timothy West

www.Oakbridge.org
Judith@oakbridge.org

The messages in this book are based on transcripts of Jeshua Evenings sponsored by Oakbridge University Press.

*Heartfelt thanks
to all, seen and unseen, who have
assisted in the preparation of this book.*

Many thanks to Ted Meske for transcribing the messages and for editorial assistance, to Tim West and Roger McGinnis for their computer expertise, and to Eva McGinnis for her loving support.

A special thanks to Charlotte Walter for her continuing friendship, inspiration and assistance in the preparation of this book.

Heartfelt thanks to the following Sponsors

Without your vision, love, support (and patience) this book could not have been published.

Royal E. Burke
Cathrine Cristof
Lawana and Don Ingle
Donald Knight
Pat and Charles Mawson
Eva and Roger McGinnis
Roberta Suzanne McMaugh
Ted Meske
Aina Pulins
Linda Pavitt Rozema
Sa'ed Sadeghi
Alvin Schultz
Most Rev. Marilyn L. Sieg
Judy Sumrell
Linda Watson
Meribeth Wheatley
ZuVuYah

In Loving Memory

DoLores and Elmer Backer
Thomas Iden Coates, Jr.
Joel Coppola
Timothy H. Cummins, DMD
Darling Robert
Tiller and Scott Finch
Genowefa and Aleksander Jarosz
Mary Catherine (The Flower)
Edward F. McMaugh, III
Sandra Pavitt Petrungaro

TABLE OF CONTENTS

Introduction	xiii
Preface	xvii
Preparation for the Shift	1
The Hologram of Life	15
The Power of Blended Holograms	27
Holograms, Realities, and ETs	37
The Ever-Changing Hologram	49
Shared Holograms	61
The Amazing Hologram	71
The Awakening Christ	79
The True Meaning of Life	89
Moving Into Light Consciousness	101
The Out-of-Body Experience	109
Connecting With Your God Self	121
The Master Secret	133
Where Do We Go From Here?	141
How Do I Love Thee?	155
The Questions Basic To Your Reality	165
The Basic Law of the Universe	179

The Expanding Universe 189
Your Robotic Self 197
Going Beyond Your Robotic Self: Tuning in to Galactic Energy 207
Do You Know How Blessed You Are? 217
Endings and Beginnings 229
Absolute Love, Infinite Light 243

INTRODUCTION

This seventh volume in the *Jeshua, The Personal Christ* series, like the previous six volumes, is filled with timeless ideas that provide gentle, uplifting guidance to experience more of the rich Inner Life within. His mind-sparkling perspectives never fail to inspire us to seek more of our long-forgotten unlimited divine nature that lies seemingly buried to our awareness, yet remains ever present within our hearts. One might think that such vitally clear messages from Christ that provide such deep insights to help us regain our spiritual heritage should be advertised under a more spiritually oriented banner than under the generic sounding name of Oakbridge University.

When Oakbridge University was chosen to be the official name for spreading this now twenty years of dedicated spiritual work, it was foreseen that Oakbridge was a strong fitting metaphor to represent Jeshua's messages. A deeper look at the word Oakbridge reveals that it is an ideal name for this work.

From tiny acorns we know that mighty oaks grow. Oak, with its long fibrous, dense grain, provides the strength to build strong bridges, buildings, etc. And letting acorns represent the nuggets of golden truth that Jeshua shares that must be lived in order to cross over the bridge from being fully engrossed in an Earthly life to experience the glorious heavenly Inner Life of the heart, the name Oakbridge University silently serves the Jeshua teachings appropriately in every way. A better metaphor could not have been chosen.

Oakbridge University tells us in its own metaphorical way that we cannot cross over the bridge by just reading truthful ideas. The truthful ideas presented by Jeshua are the ways to live our lives, and everyone is this living university. As an example: He has said many times to just be the beholder of all that goes on in the world of appearances, to see events for the illusions they are, to no longer believe the appearances to be real, especially when they are compared with the eternal Reality of peace and love, that those worldly illusions need not break our peace. Jeshua teaches many helpful ways in which to live, that when those ways are lived, they enable us to cross over the great bridge (graduate from this living university of life) that leads to the more abundant life within.

In the same manner of understanding the inner meaning of Oakbridge, His nuggets of truth are to be peered into deeply in order to fully understand their meanings so that it actually compels putting those nuggets of truth to work, so that changes for the better will carry us over the bridge to the greater Inner Life of peace and love.

With deep, deep gratitude to Judith and Tom, we say thank you for bringing forth seven volumes of the Christ teachings that literally brighten every aspect of our lives.

Don Knight, Unity minister, retired
Author: TRUE SON by Seven Arrows
(Don's spiritually given name)

PREFACE

How many times have you questioned your Earthly path? How many times have you felt separated, disconnected from the Source of your being? How many times have you entertained the thought, "Is this all there is? Who am I in the grand scheme of things? What am I supposed to do?"

There is an urge deep within that bids us look further. So we read more books, attend more lectures and seminars. Each one offers us something to contemplate, but not the whole story. Seeking the rest of the story leads us to ask questions of others, often to hear again the old concepts that no longer work for us, old beliefs we have moved far beyond.

When some answers come to us, the mind gets busy figuring it all out. Often it reminds us of all the bad choices we think we made. It finds us weak and unworthy of God's good. The mind tells us we are separate, unlovable, doomed to struggle and sickness in a chaotic world. We forget to love our self and we think we can give to others something we don't have for our self. The truth is, we can't give what we don't have.

Where will we find the answers we seek? If not in the mind, where? With the world in a state of chaos, anger, and fear, what changes do we need in order to make a difference? If all is a reflection of something within, we need to look deeper than the mind and the opinions of others to the heart. In *Absolute Love, Infinite Light* Jeshua, Jesus, encourages us again to realize that what we put out is exactly what we get back. If we put out love, love returns to us in the many ways love can. But if we fear and give in to blame and judgment of others, fear will return to us full force.

Though time is our creation, use it now to stop, breathe, and love yourself and all creation. See as God sees. Then you will see yourself and all others as perfect, whole, and complete. And, when you pray for an answer, wait for that Voice to speak. Perhaps some divine entity has a word just for you. Have we forgotten Jeshua's promise of peace, love and joy easily found when we allow ourselves to be still and know?

This book, *Absolute Love, Infinite Light,* offers so many wonderful ways to discover who we really are. It points out the value of all the changes you have chosen. All have led you to the Now of your life. Accept their gift and bless them. Great healing energies are embracing your planet. Use them wisely and lovingly. They are the gift of the Universes. Honor your divine connection. Open your mind and your heart to the wisdom of Jeshua's own words as found in the pages of this amazing and inspiring book.

Rev. Kay Hunter, D.D.
Founding and Senior Minister
The Cathedral of Light
Dallas, Texas

PREPARATION FOR THE SHIFT

Beloved one, you are one of the ones who have volunteered, a long time ago, to be incarnate at this time, to come ahead of time to pave the way and to be here now for what has been predicted and prophesied to be the great shift in the collective consciousness. It is a shift that you have prayed for, that you have tried to envision, and that you have spoken about to friends, the ones who would listen.

You have often been the master, the one who has been acknowledged as the wise woman of the village, the wise monk who knew how to access other dimensions. You have been the one who helped in birthing a new consciousness; not only birthing physical beings, but a new consciousness. So once again you are here to lead the brothers and sisters into the preparation for the shift in consciousness.

As has been prophesied, in the next few years of your timing there is going to be much of change, much that will look to you very different. You will look back upon this time and you will wonder, "How could such changes come about?" As now you look back in the last decade, the last two decades, even four or five decades back, you can see the change in the collective consciousness thinking.

In your timing of the next few years there will be as much change happening as has happened in the last five decades. So hold on to your hats, as they say, because there are going to be day-by-day great leaps of understanding. Ones are ready to shed their heaviness. Ones are ready for peace. Ones are ready to know love, to know relationships that are uplifting. Ones have been calling out for healing. They have been calling out for answers to understand that life does not have to be as hard as the world has suggested to them and as hard as the peers and parents and even friends have said to them, "Well, that's how life is."

You have already been doing much preparation for the shift. You have been awakening in the mornings asking to see miracles in the day. You have been asking to know the positive of life and being grateful for what is in your life—all of nature, all of the friends, all of the books, all of the gatherings that you are called to go to. You are finding that you are grateful for everything that happens, even if at first it may seem a little bit strange.

But you find that you know that everything works together—as I have been saying to you for a long, long time—everything works together for the realization of at-One-ment. For truly, there is only One. Everything you perceive is you, because you are bringing it forth.

Where does it exist? Ask of yourself, where does everything truly exist? In your perception, in your mind, what you see. You are projecting what you believe is possible. You are projecting it out, and then you see it as it would be in a mirror coming back to you and you say, "Okay, that must be real, because I see it." But, in truth, you have the idea first, and you are projecting it out.

So as you have been changing—and you have—you are changing your perceptions. You are changing your world, the world around you, because you are projecting a different image of what can be.

Try it on for size on the morrow. Say, when you first wake up, "I am going to see miracles in this day. I am going to see happiness, lightness. I am going to see friends who want to be in the same light space." You will notice how things fall into place miraculously, how things just happen to time themselves perfectly, and you say, "Hey, that's really cool. I like that." Be aware that very often that which you have asked for comes to you.

Be aware of the little nuances of every day, because there are miracles that happen every day. They have to, because you have set your mind to see miracles, and they come because you expect them. That is the number one ingredient in preparation for this shift: expectancy. "I expect to see miracles in this day. I expect to see Light in this day. I expect to hear laughter and to feel joyful."

If you keep your expectancies positive, that is what you will find in the day. Expectations, expectancy; that which you expect is what you are going to see. It is going to come to you. Now, I know for a long time you have been caught up in the morass of the world situation. Expect to see miracles happening there, as well. Expect to see other ones finding that they are truly able to change their lives.

I know the world has spoken that there are many who are suffering. You have projected that out because that has been old generational thinking of what you have been taught the world has to be. When it comes face to face with you—and it will—say, "No, that is not what I expect now. That is old generational thinking that I have subconsciously taken upon myself and expected to see, because the parents expected that."

The brothers and sisters that you grew up with, your peers, this is what they have expected to see, as well. And so they see it. But you are moving into a new space, and the brothers and sisters that you interact with are also moving into a new space. Expect that they will move into a new space, because they truly are. They are waiting just for that little snap of the finger to make a change.

You may speak to them of the power of expecting the good. You have had a saying some decades ago that even became a bumper sticker: **Expect A Miracle**. Well, take that as your motto every day. Expect a miracle. You can be very specific about it if you want to. "I expect a miracle regarding the balance of the golden coins and the amount of work that I do. I expect a balance in my life." You will find that it will come, because you will be asking to see it, and it will happen because you expect it.

There is truly only One. You look out, and because you have been taught to see many, you see brothers and sisters. You project out this belief. But truly, you are the One expressing as the many, and in itself it is a miracle that you can manifest such an expectation: the expectation that you are going to see hundreds, thousands or more individuals, seemingly individuals, upon the face of our holy Mother Earth.

But stop for a moment and ask yourself, "Where does that idea come from? Well, it comes from my belief that there are many people inhabiting the world. Maybe I can see this differently. Maybe there is only One of us. Maybe there is only the I, the We." We; start working with the word We, because you are joined to all of the ones that you yet see because of the belief in the many.

So start working with "We." "We feel peace." "We are happy." "We are enlightened." And then you come to a place where you begin to understand that the mind is showing you many because you have been taught that there are many. But maybe it is all a projection of the One. Play with that idea for a while and see how powerful you are.

I have spoken to you throughout the years about how powerful you are, how creative you are, how you create everything that is in your world, in your experience. You create everything. And if you create it, where does it start first? It starts with an idea in your mind. So you begin to expect that things are going to be different. "Things are going to be easy." "I am going to have everything I need."

You, as the one creative Mind that you are, will always take care of you. You can rely on that, even if you have to call on me and think that I will do miracles for you. I will, but it is truly your belief that does it. But if you want to call on me to do a few miracles for you, that is okay, too. I am happy to do that. It is easy.

Begin to understand your power. Begin to understand how Light you are, how Light everything in the world, in your world, can be as you project Light, as you feel Light. Physical lightness, yes; emotional lightness even more, and understanding that, "I expect to feel Light. I expect the brothers and sisters, as I still see the One expressing as the many, I expect to see them moving into Light."

As you work with expectancy, as you work with changing belief, it is powerful. That is why I can say to you that in the next few years you are going to be in a very different place. You are going to see your world in a very different dimension, because you are projecting what the world is.

Now, do not take, from what I have just said, guilt upon yourself and say, "People in other countries are suffering because it is my belief that they are suffering. I am guilty." No, you are not. And they are not. In truth, they are not suffering. "Oh, my goodness, how can that be true? My news media tells me that there is chaos, there are uprisings, there are military persons who are doing horrendous things. That is what my news media tells me."

In truth, they are not suffering, except as how you think they are suffering. What if you thought and expected that they are going to come to peace? Not only *might* it happen, it **will** happen. It has to happen, because you are the extension—as we have said many times—of the one creative Principle. You create everything in your life. That is how powerful you are.

The mind cannot take that all in. It can work with it, it can play with it, it can toss it around and find all sorts of objections to it. But when you work with the heart, with the feeling of the expectation, then you come to the truth. Work with loving everything that comes into your experience every day. Love it, thank it, and know that truly you have put it there as a gift.

I know many times separated ego has said, "Ha, big gift," and has wondered, "What are you going to do with this gift?" Everything is a gift which has led you to the place now where you are ready to hear that you are changing; expecting that things are going to be different; expecting that you are going to love everything in your life.

Wow, big order. It seems to be big, but you have already made great strides in moving into the space of saying, "I want to see the good in this. I am willing to see the good in this." You have already made great progress. So when separated ego will speak to you, "That's too tall an order, I can't do that, I can't love everything and count everything as a blessing," you just say back to separated ego, "Hey, I've been doing that. Where have you been? You didn't notice. I've been moving into a space of great gratitude for everything I know that I am out-picturing."

Work with loving everything that you see, everyone that you see. Work with, play with, experience loving yourself, because you are the one who is creating. You are the master, as we have spoken many times. You have heard the words and said, "Oh, well, that sounds good, but how come I have all this manure in my life?" Well, it is because you want to grow, and so you do.

Work with gratitude for what you see in your life, and then bring that back home to yourself, to loving self, and say, "Hey, you know, I've really done a good job this lifetime. I've come through a lot of challenges, worldly challenges, and I've been able to see the good in them; maybe not right away, but later on I could see the good in them." Because truly you have allowed healing in a lot of areas where at the time when you were in the middle of it you did not think there could be healing—relationships especially.

So then you live in a place of gratitude. You live in a place of saying, "Wow, there must have been a divine plan. Hmm." Then you move one step closer and you say, "I must have had an idea, a future self of me that was going to be able to look back on this and see the healing in it." Because you have in every moment what you would understand as a concept, a future self.

Play with that for a while. It is powerful. Play with being the future self of you. "What is the future self of me—and it may be like the next day or the next year or ten years—going to be doing? Where am I going to be? What do I want to be doing? What can I create?"

That is powerful, and that is part of the preparation for the shift that you are bringing about: loving self, being grateful for everything in your life, seeing everything as a miracle, being able to look forward to the future self and say, "Self, how do you see what I am going through now?"

Put it forward for perhaps twelve months. Where are you going to be in twelve months? Separated ego says, "Well, I don't know." Well, separated ego **does not** know. But the future self of you **does** know and **does** exist even in this moment, and you can access it by *expecting* to access it.

The understanding of expectancy transforms your life. It hastens the shift that has been prophesied. You believe in the prophecy and you know something big is going to happen because it has been prophesied by many, many people; therefore, it has to be true. Of course, the many, many people are projections of your belief, but it comes from the one divine Source of you that says, "It's time. It's time now to know the one Self, the one creative Energy, the One that is expressing yet as the many, the We of us.

"We are doing really well. We are bringing miracles into existence. Wow! Hey, you know, that's really great. I can speak that to the friends. You know, we are really bringing about change"—and it is true. So you speak this to the friends. Some of them will understand and be happy about it. Other ones will say, "Hmm, that's very strange." But that is all right. You have created them in order to perhaps have a bit of feedback. And in time you are going to bring about only the ones who are in the same resonance with you, because your belief and your projection is going to show you only harmony.

Like, wow! Feel that? You can feel that in the heart. The mind sometimes has a bit of a problem with it, but the heart knows. The heart feels love, Oneness. And then the heart instructs the mind to see things differently, the feeling that you just experienced of, "Like, wow, that would be so great—love, harmony, ease of living—wow, that feels so good. What if that could be true?"

The heart then sends that to the mind and says, "Hey, how about if we project agreement with friends, even agreement among nations?" That seems to be a biggie, but there is, in truth, no difference in order of difficulty. Everything is truly a miracle as you project it.

Those of you reading this have asked that you be the pivotal teachers, the ones who know what you are doing. You know that you are projecting that which you see in your life. It is what you expect to see. You are the ones who have agreed that you are going to take that power and you are going to spread it as seeds among the seeming many, and you are going to love them, because you have created them to be in your life.

You are going to say, "Wow," maybe not out loud, "I have created you. I see you as an extension of life. I see you with a body. I see you going through experiences of life. I am creating you moment by moment. In truth, there is no separation, and you really do not exist except as I see and expect you to exist."

That does not then cancel out their value. It only brings the belief system back to where it starts: to its origin, back to the one Mind which projects out. But in truth, you as individuals do not exist, except as there is belief in your mind that the other ones exist. So if you are creating them—and I say unto you truly, you are—then make them the way you want them to be. Make them as friends—happy, joyful, wanting to do things with you in a harmonious way to bring about peace, to bring about enlightenment in the world.

If, in truth, the other ones do not exist except as you bring them into your reality—lowercase "r"—then make them the beautiful beings that truly the extension of the one creative Principle would dictate that they are. Hear that well. Go back and read that again. It is true. You are creating everything you experience.

You are creating all of the friends and not-so-friends in your life. In truth, they only exist as you believe them to exist; therefore, you can see them differently. You can expect to see them differently. Now, that takes a bit of playing with, until you kind of practice, practice, practice. But it does not take too much practice before the penny drops in the slot and you say, "Oh, okay, I understand; I get a glimpse of that. Okay, and that means then that I can expect to see harmony in my world, even love." And you will.

Love is all around you all the time. It is what you truly are—love incarnate, expressing. As you understand that, you begin to feel differently about yourself. You begin to know that truly it is the power of love that dictates to the mind what you are going to expect to see, and things change rapidly.

That is why I can make the prediction that within the next few years you are going to see big changes. You are going to see big changes, because you are going to *expect* to see big changes. It has been prophesied. A master has spoken to you that it is going to happen; many masters, in truth. And you are going to project out the belief that changes are going to happen. And what will you see? Changes, the changes that you have prayed for many lifetimes.

Now you have moved to the place where you are willing to see changes. Other lifetimes you expected to live the human life with all of its challenges because you wanted to play in the sandbox; you wanted to know what that particular sandbox felt like. What color was the sand? Was it heavy, was it light, was it gray, was it pink, was it green sand? What happened when you threw it up in the air? Did it come back down on top of you, or did it fly away somewhere? You wanted to know the different sandboxes.

But in the back of your knowing, even in what you understand other lifetimes to be, there was a knowing, a hope that you would come to a place of understanding that the sandbox was just a sandbox, just a place to play; no judgment, but just a place to be creative. So you have been very creative, and now you can look back and bless every creation.

Expect a miracle. Expect to change your mind. Expect to feel differently about yourself. Expect to take on the power of changing your beliefs, and then look for the miracles, because they will be there—little ones and big ones. And that which you have thought to be difficult will find an ease in manifesting the answer. It will flow.

Change your thoughts and you change your reality. It is as easy as that. Change your expectancy and you change your reality—lowercase "r". But the power for changing your reality—lowercase "r"—comes from the Reality of the capital "R", because you are the extension of the one creative Principle. You are energy. You are Intelligence. You are the divine flow of Beingness from before time began.

You are the creators of time. And after the purpose of time has been fulfilled, you are always going to be that which you are right now—the one divine Self, the extension of the one divine Source. So if you are that—and I guarantee that you are—why not be happy? Expect to be happy, and you will be.

Understand the power of your creativity. Begin to grasp it. Begin to understand the one Mind that you are. Do not take guilt, because nothing is judged; nothing is judged. Everything serves the realization of at-One-ment. Everything brings you to the place where you are right now, where you have grasped a new idea, an understanding of how powerful you are.

Expect to see me. Play with that one for a while. Expect to see me in the light body, as a physical body glowing. Feel me. I will take your hand. Feel my hand taking yours. Reach out right now and feel my hand taking your hand. Feel the energy. Know that always, that which I am, you are.

So be it.

THE HOLOGRAM OF LIFE

I would speak with you now about how you make your own reality—lowercase "r"—and how you live within that reality and how you are not separate from your reality. I would use an example shown in one of your science fiction movies, the one known as "Star Wars," where there was shown the hologram of a sword fight, and ones in the movie were watching the sword fight as it would be right in front of them.

This is truly a good example of what you are doing. You are making a much larger hologram, inviting all of the ones to be in your hologram to play with each other, or not, and you are watching what is going on. You have invited everyone to be part of what you are experiencing. And often separated ego will say, "Well, if you are creating the hologram and you see that there is warring going on between brother and brother and sister and sister, you must be doing something wrong. You are guilty of bringing what you call the negative into the picture."

But in truth, when you stand back from it and you are in the place of Beholder, you watch how even the seemingly most horrendous acts bring forth awakenings with the people who are involved in those acts and also with ones who are watching what is happening, having it brought to them on the television screen via your news media, sometimes feeling your heart open for the ones who are enacting these parts.

There is much more that is happening beyond the appearance, and there is much opportunity for love and awakening. Oftentimes an experience that seems to be most horrendous allows one to see and feel compassion, sympathy and understanding. The heart opens and there is Oneness with the person or persons going through the experience so that you feel you are walking in their sandals.

Truly, you *have* walked in their sandals. You have experienced warfare, conflict, challenge; otherwise, there would not be the chip in your computer that registers and says, "Yes, I understand this." You *have* lived those lifetimes to the place where you now understand how it feels to be in such a situation, and your heart does open, and you reach out in worldly ways that are tangible to help ones with your gifts of different kinds.

If ones come to your doorstep, if they are neighbors and they need something, your heart opens and you share with them what you have. With ones who may be a bit farther away, you send whatever you can send; in other words, you do as your guidance tells you. In that moment there is a knowing of Oneness, a knowing that the brother/sister is walking in sandals "that I have walked in in other lifetimes; otherwise, I would not recognize it, I would not know what they are going through."

So it brings in you a knowing of Oneness. Everything—as I say to you over and over—leads to the realization of Oneness.

Every happening, no matter how it looks, has in it the potential for awakening and realizing that you are One with each other. You understand feelings. You understand journeys. You understand each other, because you have been there, no matter what one is going through. And your heart opens to support the other ones on their journey.

That is the message that I gave to you two thousand years ago, that truly you *are* your brother. You *are* the love that you seek. How could you give it to another one if you were not already that which you give? You would not know it. You *are* the love that you give to other ones, and you *are* that which you seek.

Everything is within your consciousness—everything that you see, everything that you experience, everything that you see others experiencing is within your consciousness.

There is truly only One of us having the experience that the One is expressing as many. That is Who and What you are. You are the One expressing as the many. Separated ego loves to support the belief that you are separate from each other. You look out and see different bodies, and you say, "Well, I must be separate from the other ones." But, in truth, beyond the energy of the body, you are joined in consciousness, in Oneness.

That which you would seek, you can out-picture in your consciousness. You are that powerful. We have talked about this many, many times as to how powerful you are, so powerful, so creative that you can bring your point of consciousness to the place where you say, "I am a body; I am a personality separate from others. I have talents that are separate from others. I drive a different vehicle than others do. I have different challenges, different family, different generational teaching than others do."

Separated ego loves to support that script. However, in your consciousness there is a knowing that if you will stop for a moment or so, you will ask yourself, as the computer that you are, "Where is this knowing coming from? Why do I recognize it? How can I recognize what is going on?" It is because truly, as the energy, the infinite energy of Oneness, you allow yourself—lower case "s"—to experience yourself as separate. But in Truth, you are not.

You have tested this. As you have been coming through life you have found something that you have loved or someone that you have loved, and you have lost yourself in that love. You have seen only the loved object, whether it be another person or whether it be a beloved pet or even an occupation, and you have felt the unconditional expansive love which for a moment or so does not recognize separation.

You know that you are the same energy. You love that one or that expression of self so much that you lose the limitations of who you have thought yourself to be, and you are in joy, divine joy.

Everyone has his own point of consciousness at the seemingly separate point of focus, and yet right below that, at a deeper level of understanding and knowing, it is as a stream of consciousness where you are as One, and you flow as One in the hologram that you are making.

Now, if there are things in your hologram that you want to shape-shift, you can do that. You work with allowing, first looking at what there is in the hologram as you understand your life to be, and then allowing everything to be seen as good. You have that saying in your Holy Scriptures, that God—you—made everything, and on the seventh day—in other words, the last finished day—you looked at everything and you called it good. Sometimes you have forgotten that part.

You now look at things and it is habitual—but if it is a habit, it can be changed—to look for what is wrong. You have been taught by generational teaching to look for what could be made better, what is wrong, even a small thing that could be perfected a bit. It is already perfect, but you have been taught by generational teaching—the parents, the grandparents, the ancestors have said, "Life is imperfect," and you as the small one have said, "Well, they have lived more years than I have; they must know," and so you have bought the message that was given to them down through the generations.

Seeds have been planted a long time ago, even before this lifetime, and those seeds of desire to know harmony and Oneness are growing. They are as little seedlings growing, becoming stronger, becoming more a part of your awareness. You work with this from time to time as an idea comes to you, and you wonder, "Where did that idea come from?" Well, it comes from the little seedling that was planted maybe many lifetimes ago of wanting to awaken to the place of divinity, the place that knows Oneness with All, the place that says, "I am okay," because you are, "and I want to feel that. I will start with acknowledging that for myself."

It has been habitual training to look outside of yourself to separated, individuated energy and to ask for validation from others. "If others see my worth and they mirror it back to me and they say how wonderful I am, then I must be okay. But if they don't recognize the angel that I am, the Light that I am, the little Child—capital "C"—that I am, then I must not be worthy." It has been generational teaching for a long, long time to look outside of yourself to others for validation, but there is really nothing outside of yourself.

So start with validating yourself. First thing in the morning when you wake up and you take the deep breath, know that truly you are a work of wonder that allows that deep breath to energize the body. Recognize the miracle that you are doing in that moment of focusing upon the form of energy that you have brought together called a body. Recognize the miracle that was not there a moment before that. You *are* a wondrous being, that you can bring together this hologram and call it real.

Now, your Reality—capital "R"—is what allows you to use the energy to make your reality—lowercase "r"—and to feel that this reality is true. But your true Reality is divine.

Your world is coming to a place where it is no longer being able to be so separate, one country from another. You have a global understanding. Your news media has seen to that. And your internet, your worldwide web is very good at keeping you connected with ones whom you may never see with the physical eyes, but you know what is happening with them.

You have an understanding at this point that everything looks like it is in chaos. Some of it is going through upheaval, and will continue to go through some upheaval, because you have wanted to know global harmony; therefore, your hologram, as you are making it, says, "Well, we have to have some ingredients in here of change. If it is not global harmony right now—and it is not, as it appears—we need to have some change."

So in the hologram that you are putting forth moment by moment with your consciousness, there is upheaval. But upheaval—as we have said to you many, many times—is good. It is necessary. For when you go out to till the soil, to make something as the garden or the farm crops, the first thing you do is to till the soil. You go through and you upheave it. You make the upheavals, and then you plant.

And as I have said, you *have* planted. The seedlings are growing, and you are knowing the goodness of those seedlings. Even if separated ego says, "Oh, well, you've tried this before and it's not going to work," one more time you nurture that seedling of hope by saying, "Look, I want my hologram to look different." And so, with the determination to see things differently, it happens. It has to happen.

You are the creative One, seemingly expressing as the many, who is creating moment by moment that which you experience in your consciousness. Take that deeply within the consciousness. *You are the creative One, seemingly expressing as the many, who is creating moment by moment that which you experience in your consciousness.*

As I have said, you have done this many, many, as you understand lifetimes to be, so many times that separated ego says, "Well, you have evidence that whatever you try to change for the better won't work." But where is that "evidence"? The "evidence" resides in memory, in an old computer program which, in truth, is outdated; it will not work in your computer any longer.

You have actual computer programs that are like that. They served you well for a while, and then you got a new computer or you upgraded the computer, and what happened? The old program would not run. Well, that is where you are now with the hologram that you are living. Some of those old programs do not run any longer.

That which seemingly happened to you a long time ago in this lifetime or even yesterday, where does it exist? Truly, nowhere; only in memory as you bring it up and you try to relive it. But it is not real. It is no longer real. And you, as the creative master that you are, can say unto it, "Be gone. I don't want you in my memory. You're an old program that does not serve me. I'm going to replace you with an upgrade."

As the creative One that you are, you can change anything and everything in your hologram that you are living *if* you have the will and the determination to breathe and to say, "I am determined to see things differently. Hey, you know, life is really fun. I have a lot of friends. My group of friends has been growing and expanding, and I really feel good about that. I thought I only had maybe one or two friends, but you know, everywhere I go, I make a friend. I see them as a friend, and then they *are* a friend. I have lots of friends, and I'm not afraid to go to a new place and make another friend. It is a talent that I have."

As you will see another one as being a friend in your hologram, that is what they are, what they have to be. That is how powerful you are as the creative master. You smile. Sometimes they smile back right away. Sometimes they look at you questioningly, like, "What's going on?" but it is okay. You have smiled. You have put Light into your hologram.

You have lived the lifetimes of dark holograms, enough that you know those programs. But those programs are not with you any longer, and they serve you no longer. You do not need them. You have upgraded, and you are leaving them behind. They no longer exist for you, except as you bring them into the Now reality. So you do not have to have them as companions in your holograms.

If you will understand this concept and really take it to heart, not just mentally, but really take the message to heart—that what you are living is a hologram of your making—you will begin to understand Oneness. If you will take it to heart and really feel Oneness with everyone, all of your hologram is going to shift and change; it has to, because you are the one making it. You are the one living in the middle of it.

If you could—and you can—step outside of the hologram for a moment—and this is what I have spoken of as the Beholder—to see the hologram that you are making and how one friend and another friend and another friend and another friend are interacting with you on a certain topic, in a certain way, you would begin to understand not just mentally—mentally is good, it is a good start, it has to start there first because it has been your training to start with the mental first—but then take it to the heart and feel how you are interacting with everyone and how you are part of what you are looking at, you would be in awe of what you are creating; not judgment; do not be in judgment of it.

Separated ego, because of habitual "evidence", is going to say, "Well, this hologram is not really perfect." Separated ego, again, is a program that you no longer need. You are finished with it. Look at the hologram that you are living and call it good, because it is.

Take my message to heart. Examine, as the Beholder, the hologram of what you are putting into your seeming reality—lowercase "r". Do not judge, but be in awe of what you have created.

I leave you in Love.

So be it.

THE POWER OF BLENDED HOLOGRAMS

Beloved one, you walk within your hologram not knowing that it is a hologram. However, you are now beginning to understand that you are making the hologram and that it is an illusion. You have had that description in some other writings so that you could understand that the world, the reality—lowercase "r"—is a manifestation of your beliefs, that which you could call an "illusion."

That does not mean that it is not real. It is definitely real. If you try to walk through the wall right now, you are going to bounce back, because your reality, your hologram, the generational teaching, has taught you that the wall is vibrating at a different rate than the rate of your body.

At some point in the evolution of your belief system you are going to come to a place, as I did in my lifetime, where you are able to synchronize your vibratory rate to what the wall is and to walk through the wall, because it is all energy. You are energy. The wall is energy, and you can attune yourself to it.

So do not deny the reality—lowercase "r"—that you are making, but see that it can be changed. Now, your Reality—with a capital "R"—never changes. That is the divinity of you. That is the creative Principle of you that has been from before time began and will exist after the purpose of time has been fulfilled. That Reality—with a capital "R"—is what allows you to make the holograms of the realities—lowercase "r"—and to live in what seems to be quite real and yet is a hologram.

I know that you have read in some of your texts that your reality is an illusion, and you have wondered, "How can that be? This isn't an illusion. This is for real," and it is—lowercase "r"—real. The good part of it is, because it is real—with a lowercase "r"—and because it is an illusion, you can change it. Truth does not change, but realities can and do change.

Now, when two or more are gathered together with the same hologram, wanting the same thing, talking to each other and finding resonance about the reality, there is exponential power. You are seeing this happening right now with the ones who are starting to rise up and say, "We want change." They are sharing parts of each other's holograms, and there is much power in that as they blend the holograms together and look with a shared perspective.

You have the ones who are now bringing the holograms together—overlapping is probably a good way to describe it. They may completely overlap—some holograms will. Some holograms will overlap in just one area of interest, and when they overlap, when they come together, there is resonance and there is power.

When I spoke to you two thousand years ago, I explained as well as I could about seeing each person as brother, sister, extension of the one Creator. I tried to tell you how loved you are and how you do not need to defend yourself. There were many who were willing to go into the arena and lay down the body for what they believed in order to make demonstration of changing the hologram.

And there were ones who were watching from the seats above, watching and wondering, "How can ones be so joyous about laying down the body? What is it that they know that I don't know?" Because you were willing to change your hologram and to stand up for what you believed, even though inside your mind the separated ego might be screaming, you impacted their hologram. You believed so strongly in the new hologram that was presented to you and you caught hold of it, that you were willing to lay down the body, because the body is not the Totality of you.

The body is the creation that you have made in order to walk amongst the brothers and sisters and to explore ways of knowing the different holograms and how they can be harmonious. You knew two thousand years ago that there was something much more than the body, something much more than the personality that you thought yourself to be, and you were willing to be quite joyful in saying, "Yes, if that is what is required of me, I will lay down the body," and so you did.

You changed the hologram of the ones who were watching, because they were impressed. This was a new way of looking at life: that you did not have to defend yourself or the body, that there was something greater than the body, and you gave them something new to think about and changed the world that they knew.

You are doing the same in this lifetime. You are walking amongst the friends. You have found many more now who share your ideas about what life is about and how it does not have to be a struggle. It does not have to be fearsome. It can be joyful. It can be full of happenings which you can celebrate.

Every day find for yourself something to celebrate. Separated ego may wonder if you have maybe lost your marbles, but you say, "Okay, if I lose one marble, I'll find another one." You have an opportunity then to change the way *you* look at the world and to change the way the brothers and sisters look at the world.

They begin, because you begin, to see that they have power. For too long humankind has felt powerless. They have felt that the power rested in either the appointed leaders or the royal blood. There is not any difference in any blood. There is not any blood that is more royal than yours, but there has been that belief.

For long enough you have been docile and you have allowed the power seemingly to be somewhere else, but you are waking up to the fact that you not only have power, you *are* power, you *are* the power of choice, and you are going to be exercising that power more and more until there is an evenness, a harmony, and an understanding of honor and respect for every voice.

It is a wonderful time now that you live in. It feels like—as you have a quotation from one of your books—"the best of times and the worst of times", and it is. It is the best of times because you are going through the worst of times to make yourself acknowledge the best that is in it.

You are so loved. You have not been taught this. You do not see it reinforced, mirrored back to you often. When you get with a group of like-minded ones, then you see your value mirrored back to you.

But sometimes you lose the sense of worth when you are "out in the world", and yet every part that makes up the world is divine, every brother and sister; otherwise, they would not be here. Otherwise, they would not be in your hologram. And if they are in your hologram, they are in your hologram to be loved. Take that to heart.

Separated ego may be saying, "Gosh darn, I thought maybe I could just kick them out." Love them first, then kick them out. Love them first and you may want to keep them. It is the best of times, and it can feel like the worst of times, but know that you are birthing a New Age. You have heard about the New Age for some time now and you have wondered, "Well, when is it going to come? When is it going to get here?" Well, it is here already. It is your new hologram day by day as you bring more Light into it, as you see others light up as you come to them.

Know you that feeling? You walk up to a friend and they see you and they light up. They are really happy to see you and there is a Light between you. There is an acknowledgment of the Light. This is happening more and more, where lights are getting turned on, even with grumpy old ones who thought that everything was going downhill.

Now, they may not see the Light yet, but they have a bit of hope that perhaps things might be having a potential of at some time getting better, but they think that that time is still way out there somewhere. But you are coming up to them with a smile on your face and a twinkle in the eye and they wonder, "What's going on? How come, in the midst of all this chaos and all this struggle and all these challenges and all of the negative news, how can anyone smile?"

Well, why not? It feels better than the frown. The frown only gets you a sore place in the middle of the body, and you know that one well. You know how that feels. So allow yourself to feel light. Allow yourself to smile at ones, even if you do not know them; especially if you do not know them. Smile at them as if you do know them. It will change their day. It changes your hologram and it changes theirs as well, because you have overlapped for a moment in the smile, in the Light.

And when you bring the holograms completely together where you are seeing eye to eye, heart to heart, mind to mind with each other, there is great divine power. That is what you are seeing with ones who are coming together from all walks of life, all different opinions about things, but they have a focus about wanting to be recognized, wanting to have equality so that they share at least a part of the hologram.

Maybe it is just one part, but as you start with perhaps just a small overlap and after a while there is discussion, conversation coming together and the holograms overlap, there is great, great power in that. It makes a new reality. And very soon—according to my timing, which is not always your timing (smile)—very soon you have a new world, a New Age. And that is moving and evolving very quickly upon itself, which is why you have so many prophecies about the next years in your timing, because as one choice is made for the Light, that influences another's opportunity for choice, and pretty soon you get the blended holograms of more than just two.

The new reality is contagious and it grows, and when you have the holograms of two and three and four and five and six and more coming together with the same voice, the same vision, the same hologram, sharing the same knowing that there can be change, that there *will* be change, then change happens. That is how powerful you are.

I speak to you every time about how powerful you are, the divinity of you; not as the world understands power *yet*, but the world *will* come to a place of understanding divine power—in my timing; and in yours; maybe this lifetime, maybe another lifetime.

Not all of the brothers and sisters want the same hologram *yet.* They are doing some completion with issues that they have not felt complete with yet. They have felt that they need to atone for past sins, so they feel that they have to struggle. So for a while they will struggle until finally they get tired of struggle and they will stop for a moment and will take the deep holy breath and ask, "Is there not another way to see this?" And in that moment divine inspiration comes in.

You are going to see more and more ones coming together with the same shared hologram of wanting to be recognized as equals, as divine extensions of the one Creator. Now, they will not call it by those words. They will have other words, but it will be a desire to understand and to acknowledge and to take back what seemingly they have put on the shelf for a while: to take back the understanding of their own divine power and the power of the One—capital "O"—because you see, when you get all of the holograms lined up and agreeing with each other, there is an acknowledgment of Oneness.

Nobody then has to expound upon it, because it is going to be quite obvious that they speak with one voice, from one heart. That is the power of blended holograms, and that is coming to be.

Know you how loved you are? Feel it for a moment. Take a deep breath and feel the love that is around you coming into the very heart of you, holding you as a mother will hold the new babe in arms.

Feel your heart opening and know that truly you are the Beloved; beloved of me, yes; beloved of all the masters, all the ones you still see to be separate from yourself: the guides, the teachers, the angels. You share a hologram with your guardian angel, wanting only the best for you. You share that hologram with the masters who walk with you, seen and unseen.

It is time now that you let the old beliefs in fear and struggle and unworthiness be complete and that you allow yourself to feel so loved that truly nothing else matters. You are so loved, you are the Beloved, the beloved One, always and forever beyond time.

So be it.

HOLOGRAMS, REALITIES, AND ETS

My message to you now is a strong one. Hear my message well. We will speak of the holograms and we will speak of the realities—lowercase "r"—of the illusion that you are living, and we will speak, suggest, highly suggest that you live in joy. It is a free choice, so you might as well choose to be happy.

Yes, I know the world is going to throw challenges at you, because you have devised a world that is going to give you enough challenges until the point comes where you hold your truth and you stand fast in that truth and you say, "Even this challenge is a blessing."

You are going to be offered a gift in this year, and maybe it is not going to look like a gift at first. But if you allow yourself to breathe and to feel the peace which comes with the deep breath and you can become the Beholder who just watches, does not judge, but just allows and says, "I can't wait to see how this is going to turn out," if you take that attitude, you are going to go through this year happy and you are going to know your divinity, the same as I knew that the crucifixion could happen, but I was not caught up in it. I rose above it, as you will rise above any challenge that may come in this year.

Expand your hologram, what you see as your reality—lowercase "r". Take it back to the Big Bang of your reality when physicality was created. And then, if you dare, imagine before the Big Bang. What was there before? Because there *was* a before, although it was outside of your reality of time. Allow that to be part of your hologram, as well.

Expand your hologram. Take it as far back as you can imagine: feel, create for yourself the hologram that takes in All. And when you have done that in what seems to be the past, expand it into the future. What do you want to see in your hologram of the future? See how expansive it can be. It can be anything you want it to be.

This is what I saw that evening in the Garden of Gethsemane. I saw that the cross was not the end of everything. I saw it as part of the process of human life and the process of showing that the body is a creation of your divinity, your divine Mind—capital "M". I saw myself rising, living, even with physical molecules, for years after that and having the relationships with brothers and sisters, because I enjoy friendship, I enjoy relationships with brothers and sisters. And I did this for what we have called over six hundred years until finally it was time to allow the body that I had created, re-created, to go into the Light that your divinity is.

There are even yet times when I re-create, for a short time or a little longer time, a body to come into your life, to sit next to you, to ask you, "How is it going? You look like you're struggling with something." Or just to smile and to say, "It will be okay." I have done that with you from time to time, when you have been going through something and someone has come along—maybe you knew them, maybe you did not know them—and I have either spoken through them or I have created a body momentarily to say to you, "It will be okay; not only *will* be, but it *is* okay."

You have cried, you have sobbed, and you have shouted your frustration to the heavens from time to time when you have felt desolate, abandoned. Some of that feeling of abandonment goes back to the crucifixion itself, to the time when you felt that I had abandoned you. But never can I abandon you. We are joined at the divine level as One. Never can you be where I am not. Always I am with you.

So expand your hologram. Take it back even past the Big Bang. What would that be? Can you imagine formlessness? Mind; just Mind? Just Being? There was a time, outside of time, when you did just imagine: just to Be.

And then your next question was, "What can I create?" As you are an extension of the one creative Principle, of course you are going to create, and you have created the most beautiful formations. Even in this day and time, when you look upon what is called nature and you observe the beautiful formations, watching the flow of a waterfall, the rock formations, the ferns, the glades that are green with the morning dew; you look upon the sunset, each one different from the one previous; you create. And if you have eyes to see, it will gladden your heart.

Allow yourself to put all of that beauty into your hologram and to know that truly you *are* the one creating. Would that waterfall exist if you were not there to watch it? Good question; play with that question. You will come up with an answer. Will the answer be right? Of course it will be right, because in truth there is no right or wrong; there just is.

Then allow yourself to expand the hologram and take it into the future. As long as you are drawing breath, you are going into what you call the personal future, making your future. And after you cease breathing for the body, you will still be; you will still be consciousness, and you will be—many have been—surprised. "I'm still alive! I still have and am consciousness." And you have wondered, "How can this be? I thought everything ended and I went to heaven or maybe somewhere else after I laid down the body, but I'm still alive."

Of course, you are still alive. Always you have been and will be expressing the divinity and experiencing the divinity. So expand your hologram. Allow it to be as expansive as you can imagine, and then on the morrow of the next day, play with it again and see if you can push it a little bit farther. When you do that, you come to the place where you realize, "I am expanding, I am creating, I am taking into my consciousness, my conscious awareness, more and more of Who and What I am. And if I'm doing that, hey, I'm not just a little dull piece of physicality. I must be powerful; not as the world defines power, but I must be powerful in the divine sense of creating," and you are.

In the expanded hologram you are going to remember lifetimes that were not upon holy Mother Earth. You are going to remember lifetimes when you were on other star constellations and planets, other heavenly—as they are called—bodies where you were a heavenly body. Your form may have been entirely different. In truth, it usually *was* different than what you have evolved upon holy Mother Earth.

There were the lifetimes—and I will call any form of incarnation that your creative divinity has allowed you, I will call that a lifetime, whether it be long or short—where you were liquid crystal in thought, flowing. There were lifetimes when you were very, very tall, very broad shoulders, very big, or you looked part animal, part human as you have now in what are called the mythological legends.

You have been all of your legendary beings. You have been the unicorn. You have been the one that was part female and part fish—the mermaid. You have been everything that is in your legendary stories; otherwise, it would not resonate with you. It would not be in your intellectual remembrance, your computer.

You have been everything you can imagine. You have been the tiniest little alpine flower. You have been the giant sequoia tree, living hundreds of years and watching the little humans running around doing whatever they thought was so important, as you just kept living as the giant redwood tree. You have been the fruit fly that lives for a day or so, and in that day you lived a whole lifetime.

So allow yourself to know that this is not all there is. The human form works in this reality so that you can speak with the brothers and sisters and they can understand you and relate to you so that they are not afraid because you look strange. You have amongst you ones who have come from other star constellations, not of Terra, but beyond Terra. You call them the ETs, extraterrestrials, and they are amongst you right now. Some of them have taken on human form so that you are not going to try to do away with them. You are going to maybe listen to them.

Some of you—and hear this well—are in truth the ETs. Now, I know that that blows the mind. That is good. Some of you—in fact, the major portion of you who are reading this message—are the ETs in human form because you do not want to scare the brothers and sisters, but you do want to be able to speak to them of life on other planetary bodies, and you want to allow them to understand that it is okay that there is life elsewhere.

It is foolish, hubris, pride, egotistical thinking to say that there is only life on holy Mother Earth. You are not—as the humanoids that you are—the only intelligent life. My goodness, there are some of your four-footed ones that would challenge that statement. They have more intelligence, more love to freely give than some of the human forms.

You are here because you *have* lived lifetimes on other planetary bodies and you *are* the ETs. You have that remembrance. That is why I have started off this message speaking to you of expanding your hologram and taking it back as far as you can imagine it to go and accepting yourself as being more than what you know yourself to be in this one lifetime.

How does that feel? "Well, interesting; hmm, I'll have to play with that for a while. I thought I was just human. I thought that was enough to struggle with, and now he's telling me that there's more to me than I have thought there was?" Yes. So when ones speak about the ETs among you, you know this. You can feel it as a truth within your being. It does not mean that you are going to immediately change form and have the bug eyes and the very long face, long neck, thin body, etc. that has been put forth in your so-called fiction. You are going to keep the form that is accepted, but your awareness of yourself is changing, is expanding.

Know you that is why you have felt since you were a small one that holy Mother Earth was not your home, where you have often felt that you did not quite fit in? You tried your best to be like all the rest, but there was something just a bit different about yourself. You did not know what it was, and nobody else did either, because they were not wise enough; they had not expanded their hologram.

You are expanding your hologram and allowing yourself to entertain the idea that perhaps you are much more than you thought you could be or were, much more than what the parents, the grandparents, the peers have said that you are. And as you take into your understanding that you are truly the ET, then everything changes in the way you look at things. You begin to see yourself in a new light, in an expanded Light, and you begin to invite other ETs to make themselves known to you.

Now, they may come in a form that looks human, the form that is accepted and understood, that is as a currency that ones can play with and exchange, or they may come in a different form. But because you have prepared yourself to understand that you are not tied to holy Mother Earth—you are what we have called many times a star seed—you are going to be in a place to welcome them and to ask of them, "Hey, help my memory a little bit. Where do I know you from? Where did we play together? What lifetimes did we share together? What journey have you taken, as I took this human journey and I moved into a reality that has evolved in a certain direction and you went off in another direction and developed perhaps more scientific technology, maybe more of the knowing of organic growing creativity?" You will be able to speak in a way that has a common denominator called love, a welcoming, if you will, because you will understand that you are not tied to just one planet.

Holy Mother Earth is beautiful. I have lived many lifetimes when I enjoyed holy Mother Earth and appreciated everything that we created. For indeed, we did create—as the ET that you are now understanding yourself to be. We came and brought our Light together to form holy Mother Earth. She is a Light being made out of our Light from a long, long time ago.

At first she was not the form that she is now. There was a time, even your scientists will tell you, when the atmosphere and what is called *terra firma* now was not so firm. It was more of vapor and of light—misty, maybe you could call it. And we made holy Mother Earth more and more dense. We took our Light, our creativity, and we brought it into form, and we allowed it to solidify more and more so that we could then put our creations into the seas and on *terra firma* to walk.

At first we were Light beings walking on Light, but then there was a thought to bring in density, to make more firm the Light; to change vibrational level. That is truly what we did.

Now you are starting to understand vibrational levels. You can feel vibration. You walk into a room, and if the ones in that room are happy, you can feel that vibration. It feels good; you want to be there. Or you can walk into a room where ones have been feeling very down, judging themselves and others, quarreling perhaps, and you can feel that vibration, and as soon as you have opportunity, you leave.

So you know vibratory level. It is not something that is just an intellectual term. It is something you feel, something you know down deep. And it is changing.

Expand your hologram. Go back and claim the lifetimes that you lived on other planetary bodies when you lived in other constellations. Allow yourself to know that truly you *are* the ET—extraterrestrial—living on *terra firma*, known as holy Mother Earth, meantime, so that you can bring about a common understanding that even if you meet other ETs that have different forms, or maybe not forms at all...now, there's a thought; maybe you are going to meet an ET that does not have a form, and you will wonder, "I just felt a presence. I don't *see* anything, but I felt something." It happens once in a while, and you wonder what that was all about. Maybe it was an ET. If any occurrence happens, you can access the common knowledge that you have been and are the ET as well.

There is free choice, so you can have friendships with ET vibratory energy even now. That is what you are doing when you come into resonance with other ones. You come into a group of "like-minded people" and you feel at home. It is because you *are* with ones you have known on other planetary bodies, other home bases.

Play with the ideas that I have suggested. Play with the ideas about expanding your hologram as far back as you can imagine, even past the Big Bang. Play with how it would feel to be just Mind; not to have to have any incarnate form. How would it feel to flow effortlessly? How would it feel to expand the Mind into its energetic form and know that you are energy in form, and how would you use that energy?

What kind of technology—as you would term it technology—is necessary to make a spaceship? Spaceships are energy coalesced, but you knew that already. And how did you know that already? Because you have been on spaceships, and I am not speaking that you were abducted and taken against your will. I am speaking that truly you have known space travel. Where would that idea come from if it were not true? Let that resonate for a moment.

All of your science fiction—it is not fiction, and it is not exactly scientific either—comes from a remembrance of a truth—lowercase "t"—that you have experienced, that you have created. Play with expanding your awareness of self to know that the reason that you have not felt exactly at home here is because you *are* otherworldly, you *are* the ET, you *are* the one who is boldly going where others do not even dream to go, and yet the ones who dare to dream are increasing.

More and more of the brothers and sisters are wanting out. They are feeling that this reality, the hologram that they have made for themselves, is too restrictive, and they are wanting out of it. You are the ones who are going to be exampling for them, showing them that it is okay to be a little different. It is okay to accept yourself as being more than just human.

Now, I have spoken to you very straight, and you are ready to hear it. You have asked to hear it. You have wanted to know, "Why do I feel sort of not in step? Why do I feel feelings that I can't explain?" It is because you go beyond just what is known as human. You *are* the ET. Wake up and live. That is the commission that I give unto you: wake up and live your divinity in all of its creative history and diversity. Expand your hologram, your reality, until you know your Reality, as I knew Mine.

So be it.

THE EVER-CHANGING HOLOGRAM

Beloved one, we will continue speaking of the holograms. I have used the concept of a hologram as another way of explaining your reality—lowercase "r". Your reality is—as has already been noted—an illusion. It is not real in the sense that it is not fixed. It changes.

Your Reality—capital "R"—is the unchangeable Christ spirit of you which allows you to create your hologram, the reality with a lowercase "r". However, when you are in the hologram and you have nose to window pane, you do not always know that it is a hologram, an illusion, a creation that you are making for yourself.

That is why some time ago we spoke of the importance of being the Beholder, being able to take the deep breath and to step back from whatever is going on and to ask, "What is truly happening here?" and to watch it as you would watch a play, a drama in your theater or on your big screen; to watch it from a place of non-judgment, a place of neutrality, just watching.

As you do that, as you exercise your understanding of the Beholder, you can see the hologram that you are making. Again, you will not judge it. You will see it for what it is—an experience. You have had, and will continue to have, many experiences. You are quite wealthy, and you will add to that wealth with more and more experiences within the hologram that is forever changing.

Allow yourself several times throughout the day to stop, to take a deep breath—even in the midst of everything else that you are doing or feel that you have to be doing—and try to see the experience from the place of the Beholder. Watch it as a drama. Behold your interaction with co-workers, your interaction with friends, your interaction with the four-footed ones; allow yourself to see the interaction for what it is—an ever-changing experience.

I say ever-changing, because *you* are changing all of the time. Your perceptions and the perspective from which you view everything changes momently. You add the new perception to the hologram of the illusion of the reality and it changes your belief system, sometimes by leaps and bounds, most often by a small step of change, but it does change. It is always changing.

You can step back from it and begin to realize that everything that you bring forth in the hologram is a blessing. It has divine purpose: its divine purpose is to bring you to the place where you understand that you are the One who is creating. If you do not like what you are creating, you can change it. You can just stop mid-stream, mid-thought, and ask, "How can I see this differently?"

You were born into a certain mindset of the collective consciousness. Your parents, your culture, your peers have molded your beliefs, and sometimes this molding has felt right and sometimes it has not felt right. Then you have struck out on your own and you have said, "That doesn't resonate with me. What I have been told does not feel right. I believe differently." So you have been making your own changes in the hologram as you have gone along.

Now, changing the hologram seems to be a gradual process. It seems that the process is slow. But that, again, is a belief that has been given to you: that everything has to be a process. Truly, you can make instant change. You have recordings in your holy writings of instantaneous healing, miracles of healing that I and the disciples did. Change can be quite instantaneous. Immediately, as there is change in the belief system, it changes the energy.

You are energy. You fashion your body a certain way, but if in the next day you want to have a different kind of body, the teaching has been that it has to be gradual. "Well, if I want to lose weight, perhaps I can do that over the next six weeks by going on a diet. If I want to become more athletic and be able to run faster, I can do that in a process of exercising every day and running a mile or so every day."

But in truth, you are the instantaneous being, and it is only the belief that there has to be process that keeps you from instantaneously making changes. That is what I am here to tell you. This is what I have been suggesting to you throughout the years, all two thousand of the years since you knew me as one Yeshua.

During my lifetime I changed my hologram. I knew that it was possible to change. There were times when I disappeared from others' sight, and I did this by knowing I could change my reality where they and I were no longer in a shared hologram.

I knew how to expand the hologram, and the feeling of energy, hope, knowing—truly, it was a knowing—was contagious. That is why there were ones of the multitude who caught perhaps the hem of my robe, who caught what I was saying, and instantly were healed physically—and many times mentally and emotionally—because they understood that the hologram that they were living could be changed.

As I walked amongst the multitude of people who were just like you—and if you will receive it, they *were* you; you have come back to live another incarnation and to call me forth in another way—they knew a change. They saw a possibility that things could be different, to the place where they knew that they were not the body, to the place where they could be the Christian martyrs who were thrown into the pit with the lions.

They did not have to save the body, because they knew that they were not the body, and they knew that the hologram was not real. Now, did they feel pain of the body from the lions? At first, yes, but not to the degree that they would have felt if they were in fear. They were not in fear. They were in belief that they were the creators of what they were experiencing, and they knew that they could change and leave the body behind.

You were one of the ones who caught my message in that day and knew that you were not controlled by outer circumstances and by other ones who said that they were more powerful than you. You knew your power. You knew that it came from beyond the small self. You knew that you could change your illusion because you connected with your Reality, the on-going, everlasting Reality, the divinity of you.

So I am suggesting that you play with the hologram as you understand your life experience right now to be. Play with making changes in it, because you can. You have thought that perhaps you were stuck in a certain situation and that others had power over you, but here you are, living your life day by day and not sweating the small stuff any longer.

You have chosen that your hologram is going to be a happy one and that you live in the Now; there is no other time to live, in any case. You do not worry about the morrow and you do not go back to what has been the past and judge yourself and others for what has been. You live in the Now, and that Now is always open to change. It is open to the place where you can say, "I am eternal," because you are. "I am whole, holy," because you are. "I am always being taken care of," because you are. "I will always know love," because you *are* love. "I will always have friends," because you *are* a friend to other ones. "I will always know happiness, because I choose to know happiness."

It is a free choice. You can choose to be down in the depths and to suffer, but that is no fun. You can choose to always have a joke at hand, to always look on the light side of everything that is happening. And you can choose to know divine purpose in everything that the world presents to you.

The world right now is of your making. The world right now is seemingly in chaos and making many changes. That has been the prophecy that you have made for this time—that there will be many changes—so you will see many changes, and one of those changes is going to be your understanding of your reality—lowercase "r"—and your connecting with the Reality—capital "R"—that you are, that is eternal and on-going and forever has been and will be beyond the purpose of time, because time is your creation.

Expand your hologram. Be the Beholder. Step back from it, first of all, and have a look at this beautiful hologram right in front of you of what you are doing and see how you are interacting with all of the aspects of the hologram.

See the emotions. Emotions have color. As you are watching the hologram in front of you of your reality, you can see the color of fear, the color of love, the color of courage, the color of friendship.

You can see all the various colors as they are mixing together, and you can see which ones are predominant at a certain time. You can see that as you entertain the thought that perhaps this hologram could be different, the colors are going to change. The emotions are going to change.

You have been taught down through the ages that reality is only real if you can see it, touch it, taste it, feel it, smell it, etc. But you are the one who is putting the parameters on the hologram, and you can change those parameters. Imagine a hologram, your hologram, on the floor beside you. You can say, as the Beholder, "Look at the way I'm worrying about something that doesn't really exist." That gives you a new perspective. "I think it exists. Look at those colors. Wow, look at that red. I'm really angry about something. Oh, now it has changed to green because I understand that it was rage. It really came from other lifetimes, and it has nothing to do with this present hologram, so now it's green. It is healed."

Play with being the Beholder. Imagine. You have built into this reality—lowercase "r"—the most wonderful gift of imagination. It is fun to watch the hologram on the floor and see the colors as they change and to see how certain other persons come in and what color they bring with them.

Imagine. Be the Child, the Beholder Child that looks at the hologram and then says, "Hey, I can change that. Wow! Okay, this *is* the time for change. I thought this meant that other people were going to change; world affairs were going to change. I didn't know that it actually meant that *I* was going to change my hologram, that *I* was going to understand that I am not controlled by anything beyond my belief system. I am in charge of my hologram. I can change that. Wow! I was really worrying about the golden coins. Ha! I don't need to. I see ones coming in who are the green color who want to support me. Hmmm. Jeshua has said that I'll always be taken care of,"—and you will.

You will always be taken care of. You will always have raiment to wear and a dwelling place, and it is going to get better. "Wow! That's a great thought. It's going to get better. This that I have right now, it's pretty good. Sometimes there are a few things I would change about it," you say, "but Jeshua says it's going to get better."

Yes, it is going to get better, because you are going to understand your power. You are going to understand that the hologram that you have been struggling with is just that; it is a hologram, it is very malleable, changeable; it can be shaped, molded, and changed.

Now, one of the things you are going to want to do besides taking the deep breath and being the Beholder is to get some clarity about what you want in your hologram. You are going to take out your notebook paper and you are going to write down how you want your hologram to look, what you want the aspects in the hologram to look like. Be very definite, because you can be. Take for yourself the appointment book and put in time for yourself.

You are a giver. You are a lover. You want to give. You want to make it better for other ones, because it makes you feel good to see other ones feeling good. You have "learned" this from other lifetimes and in this lifetime. You live in love and you want to love other ones, and you are free to do this.

They may or may not meet you on the same energetic level. They may or may not accept your love, but it does not matter. You can go on loving them. They cannot stop you from loving them. You do not always have to be in their presence, but you can keep on loving them, and they cannot do anything about that; that is your choice to keep on loving them. But as I have said, you do not have to be in the same room with them if it is uncomfortable. You can love them from a distance, and sometimes that works better.

The concept of the hologram is powerful. When you begin to understand that your reality is right here in front of you and you watch it as you would watch a play, a drama, the instant that you know you are the one who is making this hologram, everything changes. It has to.

You have done really well up to this point with living in your reality. You have your challenges, yes, but you also have the successes. You can look back over this life and say, "Well, that was really a hard time for me, but you know, I came through it. I wasn't really happy when such and such happened, but I overcame that. I came to the place where I accepted it. Maybe I still wasn't happy about it, but I could be okay with it."

You have the times that you can go to where you have been successful, and I highly suggest that you bring those to mind and you live in that energy. Remind yourself of every challenge that you have come through and all of the successes that you have had.

Do not dwell on the other ones where you have been judged or you have judged yourself, but get into the feeling of positives, the feeling of success, the *knowing* of success. Go with a light step, living and loving everyone who comes into your experience, everyone who comes to mind, whether they are activating a body or not.

When you release the body, you do not release the consciousness. You are always that which you have always been—energy; divine energy, conscious energy. Always you have been conscious energy, but sometimes you have had the blinders on and you did not recognize it. You have had the past teaching—and it has been reinforced by the parents and the grandparents and others—that when you lay down the body, you either go to a very nice place and you get to play a harp, or you get to go to the place where you can roast marshmallows.

But that is just a teaching, another hologram, another belief, and very soon the loved ones move past that old teaching, that belief, and they call unto you. They say, "Hey, wake up."

You are now all that you have ever been and all that you will ever be, because you are divine energy right now, and you can change the hologram that you are living in and you can expand it to the place where you know that you are divine energy and that you create moment by moment by moment.

You do not even have to have the body—now, there's a thought. You do not even have to have the body in order to know the feeling of success. "Wow! You mean I am forever on-going? I'm not just tied to this timeline right now, this body right here, this experience?"

No, you are forever on-going, and when you get finished with the body, you are going to still be making experiences for yourself. If you start now—which I highly suggest that you do—in understanding that you are creating the hologram, think how powerful you are going to know yourself to be when you do not have to look after the body and drag it around. You are going to be free; free energy.

The purpose of my lifetime two thousand years ago was to demonstrate that you are not constricted by the body. I released the body in one of the seemingly most tortuous ways upon the cross, and it was done that way on purpose—to show you that you are not the body. You create it moment by moment by moment, the ever-changing hologram.

That is what this time is about. It is not about the changes in the outside world. They are going to change, yes, because you are changing, and they are going to be in upheaval for a while because you have believed that that is the only way change can come, but that is not the only way that change can come.

Change can come easily with a deep breath and a new belief, with the energizing knowing that, "I Am everything, all things, every thought; I Am divine."

Always you are loved with an everlasting love. Always I love you. Always I am suggesting that you change your hologram, your illusion, your reality. Expand it. Bring into it the positive energy of success, of knowing how powerful, how loved you are.

So be it.

SHARED HOLOGRAMS

The changes that come now are ones that you have set in motion some time ago, in this lifetime and in previous lifetimes, because you have wanted to know the holy Self of you.

So whenever changes come, welcome them and say, "Okay, as the Beholder, I stand back and I watch to see how this plays out." Remark on that word; listen to that word—how this *plays* out; not "how this is going to trip me up", but "how this plays out." It is a play within a play within a play, and you have made great dramas. You have lived through many, many dramas that separated ego said would extinguish you, and yet here you are.

You are making your realities, your holograms. You are making the illusion that seems real, because you are creative. There is nothing wrong in making the holograms. They are not to be judged. You are proving to yourself that you are the creative One, so it is good as far as it goes.

As you will contemplate what you want to have in your hologram, in your reality, you will be surprised, for answers will come, people will come as an answer perhaps to a question. And you will find that the pieces that you have thought to be far away and hard to find will come to you. You can trust that, because you are creating moment by moment the Now moment, and each Now moment is perfect in itself.

Now, as we spoke about the individual holograms, the illusions of reality—lower case "r"—we touched on the shared holograms where you feel that you are in somebody else's reality as well as your own, and they are in your reality as well. You have devised this most wonderful way of understanding the One—capital "O"—that you are. For you are the One expressing as the many.

You have decreed that you want to see yourself from all aspects, and so you have created the tall ones, the short ones, the big ones, the small ones, the intelligent ones—seemingly, by human standards—and the ones who are a bit more simple. You have fashioned a hologram that takes in All, and it seems to be a shared hologram.

You invite ones to come into your hologram, into your reality, and you feel that they are sharing the hologram with you. Now, in truth, it is your reality, and they do not really exist as separate from you. In truth, it is your hologram, expanded. In truth, there is only One Reality, and it is the divine holy essence experiencing and expressing as the many.

It does not need to change how you want to make your hologram. Just understand that as absolute Truth, there is only One, and the rest, as they are seemingly individual, do not exist as separate from you.

This is something that I discussed with my masters and teachers. It is a way of understanding that the hologram that you make does not, in truth, have boundaries to it, does not have limitation. It allows you to move beyond human mind into Mind, which is what I allowed myself to do: to know the Truth of my being, which is the Truth of your being, because we are One.

The great I Am, which is you, is creating a reality that seems to be populated by many individualities. And as I have said, you do this for the purpose of knowing the aspects of yourself. You want to know, "How would it feel to have long hair, short hair? How would it feel to have many golden coins? Hmm, oh, I like that one. How would it feel to be the happy one who knows that he/she is always taken care of, doesn't have to worry about anything? How would it feel to know that I am the one who is always going to be living in love and in appreciation and in the divine knowingness of the Essence that goes beyond human knowing?"

It can take you into a very exalted state. It can take you to a place where you see the drama of the world and you see the interactions of brothers and sisters, and it allows you to go even further beyond that: to acknowledge the drama, yes; to take part in it if you want to; and it allows you to know that this is not all that you are.

Your hologram, your individual hologram is not all that you are. Thank goodness, hmm? You *are* the One expressing as the many, the many aspects of what humans can be, how they can react with each other, how they can love each other, how they can be hurtful to each other, and how they can heal all relationships.

You are very powerful. So when you sit with that idea and you realize, "I am much more than I ever knew myself to be," there is great freedom, great power to know your Self—capital "S"—to move beyond the human perceptions.

What if you had the belief that you were as the great whales or dolphins and you could swim in the water? And you could allow yourself to rise up out of the water and walk with your tail on the water and then flip over and back into the water as you have seen the various aquatic animals do? Where would be the fear of walking on water? It would be an unknown thing. There would not be fear.

What if you knew that you could make yourself appear and disappear according to your wish? Actually, you do this already, but again, you do it in process which seems to take some time. But already you do this, because you appear somewhere and you interact with people, and then you leave and you have disappeared. It is just a matter of perception and the belief in time.

If you want to do it more quickly than that, all you have to do is change your belief about what you can do and how you can do it.

So if you want to make changes—and this is a good time for changes—start. Do not wait for me to do it for you. I cannot. Do not wait for somebody else to give you permission, because truly no one else can give you permission. You have to decide what you want to do, and then you do it.

You do make preparation. You think it through, because it makes it a little easier if you have a clue, at least a beginning clue. But you start. You do not have to wait. If you truly desire something—now, that is a big "if"—you will contemplate what I am saying to the place where you understand that if you truly desire something, you will manifest it.

Many of you have intuitive sight; in other words, you can look to the future. And you get impatient. You say to me, "Jeshua, I want it right now." Well, you can have it right now, but perhaps you will have to readjust some of your perspective and allow space for process, as there is yet belief in time, and know that it is in process.

Separated ego is not always comfortable when you want to make changes. Separated ego will say, "Well, I want to hold onto a few things yet before I make the big leap." Okay, and there is nothing wrong with that. There is no judgment. There is no big referee that says you "should" be doing it right now. It is up to you and your Self—capital "S". That is why I have suggested you ask Self. "Self, what do we want to be doing? Where do we want to manifest our Light? How do we see the next Now moment or the next Now decade?"

Ask your Self, "What would bring me joy?" That is the true purpose of life. Ones have asked, "What is the meaning of life?" **The meaning of life is to be in love with life.** "Oh, well, that's a bit too simple. To be in love with life, to be happy with where I am and the friends that I have and what I'm doing? Well, separated ego tells me that I should be painting the house, making a few changes to the body, or whatever."

But that is separated ego, and it is always going to come up with ways to "improve" yourself. You are perfect as you are. You need not try to make yourself *more* perfect. It is truly impossible. You are already perfect. It would behoove you to accept it and to know, "I, of myself right now, am perfect. I am okay. I can move forward. I can do that which I want to do with ease, right now."

That brings a sense of power—divine power—to you that tells separated ego that you honor it for the help it has given you in times when you felt it was necessary, but in truth, you do not need it any longer. All of those fears that you have had through the years, what have they brought you besides some stress, worrying about things, and some sleepless nights?

Okay, you have been there, done that. You can check that one off the list; been there, done that. If you have things you want to do while you are still moving about in physicality, get on with it. Do what you want to do. If it is to jump from the big bird and to feel and remember how it feels to fly, how gravity seemingly has power to bring you back to Earth again, do it. If you want to walk on water, start with a puddle…or some ice cubes. If you want to demonstrate happiness, smile. That is all you have to do.

Separated ego will say, "Well, you have to do X, Y, & Z first in order to be happy." Actually, no. All you have to do is smile, and that sends a message throughout the body, and all of the cells respond and know that you are happy because you are smiling. Or you get into what is called the silly mode, and you laugh about something and it becomes contagious and someone near you sees you laughing and they do not know what you are laughing at, but it must be funny, and so they catch on and they start laughing, and pretty soon someone else down the line starts laughing and they do not know what they are laughing at, but everybody else is laughing, and it is contagious.

Have you ever been there? Of course, you have. It does feel good, and it does a body good. All of the cells get a little bit shaken up into a good place, especially with a good belly laugh, and they get to feel expansive. That is why I speak with you to see the Light that you are and to allow every cell in the body to come alive in that Light. Allow them to know that you are free, that truly anything you want to manifest, you can manifest.

You do not have to wait for my permission. I give it to you. Okay? Permission granted. Now, I have taken care of that. You do not have to wait for the golden coins. "Oh, that doesn't make sense, Jeshua. I have to have the golden coins; otherwise, how can I proceed?" Well, you start by seeing the process going forward. Perhaps you do not have to have the golden coins. Perhaps you can do it with the plastic [the credit cards].

Know you that your plastic is a miracle? Know you how much power you give the plastic? You believe that it has value. It comes down to belief. There are actually no golden coins there in that piece of plastic. There is no tangible gold or silver that you can build something with, but there is trust, there is belief. You use the plastic all of the time because there is belief that it is much easier than lugging around heavy suitcases full of golden coins. But that is what the piece of plastic stands for, and because there is belief in its worth, it is acknowledged to have value. It is supported by belief; the same with your paper.

You are powerful. I keep telling you this so that finally sometime you are going to wake up in the morning and say, "Self, what do we want to do today? Because, you know, Self, we can do anything we put our mind to. Anything we believe, we can do, and we can do it easily. It doesn't have to be difficult."

That is a big one, but it is possible. Otherwise, you would not be reading these words. The messages that I give to you,

I call forth from the one Mind that you are. Oftentimes you will say afterwards, "How did he know what I was thinking? How did he answer my question before I even asked it?"

How could I not, when there is only One of us? I love That Which you are. I know That Which you are. I see the changes that you are making and will continue to make. I see how you are going to enjoy this year. You are going to look back on this year and you are going to say, "Wow! I didn't know that I could do so much." And it will seem like a miracle.

And truly, the Awakening *is* a miracle. You deserve the Awakening. You have been asking for it for a long, long time. You have been putting it in process. You have decreed that there is going to be an Awakening. "I'm going to awaken to my power, my divine power. I'm going to awaken to the place where I know I am the Christ, the divine Self going forward. I am going to look at the drama of the world, I am going to be aware of it, and I'm going to send my love to the places that seem to need it. When ones ask me to keep them in mind in my holy vision, I will do that, because I know that they are whole."

You are going to awaken in this year. Hear that well.

There is a light that shines brightly. It is a hope that is going to be fulfilled. There is a Light that you have been living for a long time, and it is going to come in its brilliance in the hologram that is shared by the many aspects of yourself. And when that day comes, which is not afar off, remember the One of us, and rejoice.

So be it.

THE AMAZING HOLOGRAM

Beloved one, you create a miracle in every moment. You bring the focus of your consciousness so completely to what you believe to be your reality that you temporarily exclude the Allness of you and you walk in the hologram you call your reality. You say, "This is my reality. This is who I am. This is the employment that I have or that I am taking a vacation from. I am defined by my family, my ancestors, even by my descendants. I am defined by all that I experience." By focusing so specifically upon the present hologram, you temporarily forget the All of you.

As you put a focus upon your employment, profession or your family, it is important to you and it defines you for a time, but it is not who you are and it does not define you to the exclusion of your Reality. In Truth, the Reality of you is what allows you to fashion the experience you call reality.

You have certain interests that you like to follow, and they add to your description of who you feel yourself to be. These interests, passions, change from time to time, because you have decreed, as the holy Child that you are, the expressive One come forth from the divinity of you, that you will experience a myriad of adventures.

Your hologram is the most wonderful extension of you. Creativeness is you. You are very creative, and you have seen this as you have come through the various stages of life this lifetime and other lifetimes. You have seen how creative you can be. You have been creative in bringing forth the friends and the ideas that you throw around with the friends like in a certain game. You have an idea and you toss it to another one and you say, “What do you think about this?”

They play with the ball and they throw it back to you, or they may throw it to another friend. After a while, when it comes back to you, it looks a bit different than it did in the beginning. For in truth, if you could see one of your sports items such as the basketball and could actually see all of the fingerprints that have ever been placed on that basketball, you would see that it is a world in itself. Everyone who has touched it has left their imprint on it.

It is the same with an idea. You have an idea. You put your imprint on it and you toss it to someone; they catch it and they put their imprint on it, and then they throw it perhaps to another one and they add their imprint.

You play with the ideas, and sometimes you integrate them into your hologram and they change the hologram until it is different than it was the day before or a year before.

Now you are wanting to know, "What is Reality—capital 'R'? Who am I? What am I? *Why* am I? How do I work with spirit to the place where I know myself to be as the drop of water in the ocean, a drop of consciousness in the All That Is?" There are times when you are in meditation or when you are first waking up in the morning before you are totally focused on the day when you get a feeling of Allness, of non-separation.

Now, I know there are many who, as soon as the eyes are open, are focused upon this reality. Allow yourself a moment or so when you first wake up to spend a little bit of time that the world does not own, a little bit of time when you can look at the hologram of what you have thought yesterday to be and what you have thought that this day that you are waking up to is going to be, to the place where you can see yourself going forward in the day in love, in peace, in joy, knowing and affirming that everything in this day works to the good for you.

You will find that that day *will* work for the good of you. Even if something that previously you would have called a snaggle happens, you will say, "Well, I have decreed that everything in this day works for the good for me; therefore, this has to be good. Now, where is the good in it?" And you will find it. You will find that it has a silver lining.

Even if you are sharing the bed with somebody, allow yourself to stretch out and to take the deep breath and inhale the spirit that you are. Inhale the joy that you are. And then when you get to a certain place where you feel really good about yourself, not worrying about who you have to see or what you have to do or how much you have to get done in that day—knowing that you are always being taken care of, you are always being guided—then you can leap out of bed ready to face the day; not only to face it, but to enjoy it, to interact with it as the creative divine One that you are, making that day as you go along.

In Truth, every day is unwritten until you start to write it. Now, you have tested this for yourself. There have been some days when you thought you had to do such and such, and then something happened and you did not do those things. You re-wrote the script for that day. Perhaps there was a telephone call that changed everything and the whole day was rearranged and you rewrote that day. *In truth, no day is written before you write it.*

There is a miracle that you use in writing each day. It is called the miracle of choice. It is the Master secret and we will speak more of it later. You always have choice. You are free to write every day. It is interesting when you get to the end of a day and you look back on it and you say, "Oh, that's interesting. I didn't know he was going to call me. I didn't know that this was going to come in the mail for me. I didn't know that an opportunity was going to come, one that I didn't even know existed, but this opportunity came today. There have been certain things I've been hoping for and wishing for and they've been taking their time getting here, but today they got here."

So remember that each day you are re-writing, creating your hologram of that day. If you want it to be expansive, it can be as expansive as you allow it to be. You can write into that day whatever you want to write in, with no judgment, only the freedom of choice. You will find that this sets you free from the world.

In every moment you have choice. I am not just saying this because it sounds good. I am saying it because it is true. And you will know it as you use it, as you practice it. Every day you make the hologram that you live within.

If for a moment or so you slip into another dimension—and I have seen you do that in meditation, or even as you are doing some of the household chores that do not take all of your attention and you let the mind wander—you change your hologram, your reality, because you have opened up a window in it that allows something new.

Practice opening up the boundaries of what you have thought to be true. Sometimes you have said, "This is my truth; this is all of it and I'm staying with it because I know it; I don't like it, but I'm staying with it because it's mine." Well, you can make something else yours, because you have choice.

The hologram is a reality that you live within as you believe it to be true, and you can expand it in any moment.

For example, right now, imagine yourself to be in a garden. Look around. What flowers do you see? Are they short? Are they tall? Is there grass? Are there trees? Are there birds in the trees?

Okay, come back. For a moment you changed your hologram. You made a side trip off to a peaceful garden. Perhaps you saw tall flowers. Perhaps you saw short flowers; different colors. Perhaps you saw small birds, perhaps large ones. You can return to that garden any time you want to, by choice, even if you are right in the middle of a toe-to-toe "agreement" with a co-worker who is describing the 1, 2, 3 of what has to be done.

You can breathe and go to your garden; eyes open. "Ah, I'm in my garden. Oh, yeah, okay, yes, I hear you; okay; 3; okay." And do not worry if you miss the first two, because usually whoever is counting off the 1, 2, 3 of what has to be is going to repeat himself; that is human nature.

Never do you miss anything. Your hologram is often like a sponge. It can take in whatever you choose to take in. You do not have to take in the muddy water. You can take in the light, the light water, the clear water. Your hologram is like the sponge, and even sometimes without thinking about it, you absorb what the world wants to give you.

As each day is unwritten until you write it, your future is unwritten until you write it. If one door seems to be closed—or two or three—look somewhere else. There is always a blessing in everything, even if it seems to be a little bit hard to find, even if it takes a bit of patience, even if it seems that "no matter what I try, it never works".

I know you have felt that way. That is the human understanding. "No matter what I do, it never works." And then one day something works, and you say, "Oh, my God—truly, oh my God—things have changed." And who has made them change? You have; by choice, by *believing* that you have choice, and by acting on that choice, and being happy in each day even if that which you have been "programming" has not quite come to you yet, having to exercise—remark on that word, exercise—patience.

Using patience gets easier the more you experience it, the more you exercise it. You get to the place where you say, "Well, it hasn't happened *yet*, but the desire is out there, the intent is out there, and it *will* happen. Meantime, I'm very happy with whatever I am doing." Because if that which you have programmed has not happened yet, you are free to enjoy where you are, and you do not have to hurry up and do something else. You can enjoy just breathing.

When you awaken in the morning—those extra few minutes that you give to yourself—breathe, yawn, expand the body, expand the lungs, especially for those of you who are the side-sleepers and you are compressing the lungs during the night. Throw open the arms and allow the lungs to expand, and breathe deeply. The body will thank you for it.

No matter how you sleep, allow yourself to expand with stretching the muscles and wiggling around a bit as you first sit up in bed. Wiggle the toes. Toes have not been wiggled all night unless you have had certain dreams where they have been very busy. But for the most part, toes have not been wiggled during the night, so allow them to wiggle, to exercise a bit. Every part of the body, stretch it out. Invigorate the body with breathing, with allowance, and with choice, and remember that the hologram of that day has not been written until you write it.

So be it.

THE AWAKENING CHRIST

We have spoken over the years of many concepts, bread crumbs as they would be, leading you to the place where you find yourself now in your understanding of Who and What you are. We have given you clues along the way, ideas to play with, concepts that have expanded your mind and your understanding; questions sometimes which allow you to think so long and so hard that finally you have tired of thinking and you have allowed the heart to know the answer; in other words, to feel the peace and the joy of the Christ.

Each time you choose to acknowledge the Christ power of you, you change the vibratory rate of the collective consciousness and you allow it to ascend. Truly at some point the collective consciousness is going to awaken and it is going to feel an ascension. Sometimes the bodies will feel it also and there will be the physical ascension, but that is not the important goal. That can happen, because you will come to that "Aha!" place where everything dissolves into Light and you no longer need/want the body, and you are so Light that you ascend. But that is not, as I have said, the goal.

The goal is to awaken to the place where you have the divine moment and you know, truly know, "I Am That Which I Am, that which I have always been. I Am the Christ, and I celebrate the Christ of me and—because there is no separation—the Christ of everyone I meet."

Everyone you meet you have invited to be in your consciousness, to be in your awareness. Everyone you meet is of the same energy and the same fabric that you are. Everyone is the Christ, whether they know it or not. And you, as the days go by, are going to be recognizing more and more Christs walking, interacting with you, to the place where you are going to be smiling and welcoming them.

We have been speaking in previous times about the changes that are happening. We have spoken of the divisiveness, where that which is not of Light is showing itself and inviting the Light to shine upon it.

You are at a place where you will be feeling the changes; some of them will feel good and you will understand them. Some of the changes will require that you take a deep breath and stand in the neutral place of Beholder for a moment or longer in order to see how they might lead to the atonement, the realization of at-One-ment.

Sometimes you are going to have to take more than one deep breath. So I would suggest unto you that you collect unto yourself, as many as is possible, ones of like mind who support your knowing of the Christ, who support your belief system and the molding and shaping and changing of that belief system as they mold and shift and change their belief systems.

As often as is possible, seek out the ones who are of like mind. Now, I know that you are going to be walking amongst the brothers and sisters who may not use the same language or who may not have the same viewpoint. You will love them and you will be with them, but as often as it is possible, seek out the ones who are going to be of like mind to support you as you support them.

You are very strong, so it is not going to hurt you to be with others who have differing viewpoints, but you are going to want to come back to a place where you can let down some of the armor which you have put on for many lifetimes and just be with friends because they love you, they understand you, they know what truly is happening; not what appears to be happening, but what is truly happening. Some of the changes are going to be great. They are going to be all for the good, even though at times they may not look that good. If you are with friends and you can affirm that, "This, too, shall evolve into the realization of the whole Christ," then whatever is going on is going to take on a different appearance, quite literally in some cases.

There is truly nothing to fear. Hear that well, because once you take hold of that idea, that Truth of your being—that there is nothing, truly nothing to be afraid of—fear loses its power. Fear has been your companion many lifetimes, and you have learned how to armor yourself because you thought there was something out there which was stronger than you.

First of all, there is nothing "out there". It is all within your consciousness. In addition to that, there is nothing that you can bring forth that is going to harm you, because you are the one who is creating it. And if you are the one—and I guarantee to you that you are the one creating it—you can un-create it as soon as fear is banished off to the wings, off stage, no longer necessary.

Fear is not a Truth. It is the truth with lowercase "t", but it is not True with a capital "T". Fear is something you have created in order to adventure, to have the rush of adrenaline. There is nothing outside of you and there is nothing that you need defend yourself against.

One of the big changes that is coming *is* the letting go of fear. Fear no longer has power over you. It only has power as you give it power and think that it might be True, but it is not.

The only Truth of your being is that you are energy, energy that I have called Love. I have likened that energy to love, because when you are in love, you feel expansive. And when you are in love with someone, you forget the small self and you are only interested in the other one. For a moment or longer you find yourself forgetting yourself and the armor that you thought was necessary, and you feel yourself to be One with the person who stands before you. You know only Love.

Love is expansive. Love is energy, and you are energy. You have always been energy, and you have always had choice how to use that energy, how to fashion and form it. And then as you have created, you have found yourself enamored with your creations to the place where you felt that you had to defend those creations. You have felt that perhaps something could come along and knock over your sandcastle or whatever you had created, and so you began to identify with your creations to the place where you have forgotten that you created the creation in the first place.

That has been called "the fall from grace," the fall from the remembrance that, "I am the divine One who created this in the first place." That has been the fall into density, and now you are ascending out of it because you have had enough. You are not vulnerable. Never does the holy Child need to be defended. The holy Child is not vulnerable. The holy Child is Energy.

Now you are in the place where you are awakening to the Christ of you, awakening to the place where you know your power; not as the world dictates power. That is in a duality. In the world, you can have power one day and lose it the next, seemingly.

The true power of you lies in your realization of the Christ of you that has never been lost. You have had a lot of adventures, but you have never been lost. Furthermore, you have never sinned. You have made choices and you have lived with the result of those choices and have gone on to make other choices, but in Truth, verily, you have never sinned. You have played, the same as you will watch the little ones as they play in the sandbox or they play on the different equipment. They make choices. Perhaps they climb up the ladder and maybe they fall down. But they get up, brush themselves off, maybe they cry a little bit because they want somebody to acknowledge who they are and that something has happened to them. And then what do they do? They run off and do it again quite often. You have done the same thing in lifetimes. You have gone through adventures.

You are not just the body. In fact, you are much more than the body. When your scientists measure the aura, which they are now doing, they see that you are not ending with the skin. The skin is part of the body. It is one of the organs of the body. It happens to be on the outside. But the physical is not all that you are, and the body is not activating itself. You are activating the body, and the Light that you are is extensive.

In truth, the divine energy of you, the Christ of you extends even farther than you can imagine. You are part of the cosmos itself. The cosmos, the constellations, all of what your scientists are now bringing to your awareness, is there only because of you.

I am putting out ideas for you so that you can understand that you have nothing to fear. As one wise person said, "There is nothing to fear but fear itself." Once you come to the realization that there is nothing to fear—and there is not—you are free. You do not have to worry about the body letting you down. You do not have to worry about friends, co-workers, employers letting you down. You do not have to worry about the leaders and the government letting you down. You can let them go off and play their own games, because your belief system, your consciousness knows that you are okay and will always be okay.

You do not need the employment, someone else giving you directions so that you can earn the golden coins. If you were not in that employment, you would be serving somewhere else, because that is what life is for: to love, serve, and remember. So if you were not where you are, you would be somewhere else serving and loving, and there would be an exchange of energy because there has to be. There is never a vacuum. There is always an exchange of energy.

Now, I am not saying for you to go in on the morrow or the next and say to your employer, "Hey, I don't really need you any longer. Jeshua says I am free to make my own choices, so I think I'll just leave." I am not saying that at all. I am saying to appreciate where you are and to understand and know that you serve willingly. And yes, there has to be an exchange of energy. Nature, the true being of you, does not allow for a vacuum. There has to be an exchange of energy. So anywhere that you go, anywhere that you serve, there is going to be an exchange of energy. It may be in the form of the golden coins or it may be in another way, but always there is an exchange.

Your responsibility is to be aware that there is an exchange and, even though it may not look like the golden coins, there will be an exchange; there has to be an exchange. Nothing is ever done in a vacuum. And then you begin to realize that the ways that you are being paid, the exchange of energy, can be as varied as the grains of sand on the beach—many, many different ways it can come back to you, and will.

You will never be without. Sometimes it may look a little bit tight, but never will you be without. Always you will be taken care of, because you have ordained that you will be taken care of.

You will never be lost. Ones fear laying down the body because they question, "Where do I go? Will I still have consciousness? Will I be lost, adrift in the void somewhere?" No, you will always have consciousness. You will always know yourSelf—the greater Self, capital "S"—and in fact, many who awaken after having released the body feel very joyful because they are free. They expand.

The light at the end of the tunnel is your own light, and you expand into that light. There is nothing to fear. Now, I am not saying that message because you are going to release the body soon. In fact, you are not, because there is much work to do. The harvest is great, and the laborers are very much needed.

So you are not going to lay down the body while there is still work to do. But when you come to the place of knowing completion with this incarnation, there is nothing to fear. It is only going to be all joy, Light, expansion—but not yet, because I need you to do my work. You are my hands, my feet, my smile, my words of comfort to ones who cannot see me, who maybe do not have yet the belief system that will allow them to know that they are not alone.

Some of them call out to me and to my mother, Mary, and they want to know comfort. But when we answer—and we are always there with them, with you, each and every one—they do not hear us, because a long time ago they were told that they were not worthy to know Oneness. They were not worthy to have their prayers answered. If they did not pay the priests and rabbis and make sacrifices in the holy temple, then their prayers did not amount to anything. You were taught that in many lifetimes.

So when we answer, they think it cannot be, because they still see me upon the cross. I am not on the cross. I only stayed there for a few hours. That was long enough. Then I came down from there, resurrected the body, knew it to be energy, and walked amongst you again to prove, to show to you that you are Life itself. It cannot be extinguished. I will not be extinguished. Life may change form, but Life itself cannot be extinguished, so there is nothing to fear; you only know joy.

You are Life; always have been, always will be in one form or another; always serving the Light, because you are the Light and you recognize That Which you are.

And you recognize other ones who are beginning to awaken to the Light that they are. You celebrate the Light with them. That is why I say to you, seek out ones of like mind and be with them as much as is possible, because the feeling of Light and the awareness of the divinity of you expands as you reaffirm the Truth of your Being.

If you surround yourself with—I will use one of your words here—negative people, you know how that feels. It feels heavy, constricting. That kind of energy has yet to awaken to All that it is.

So as much as is possible, seek out ones who are ready to have joy in their life, to know innocence, to play, to laugh, to sing, to celebrate truly the awakening of the Christ. It is the awakening Christ who reads these words. You have foreordained that at some point in linear time you will know the Christ of you, and this is the time.

So be it.

THE TRUE MEANING OF LIFE

Beloved one, many times, throughout various lifetimes, you have sought me. You have wondered, "Where is the divine magic that I knew when I was with Yeshua? Where is that love?" And in seeking, you have served me every lifetime in the various religious/philosophical orders, the lifetimes when you were the humble peasant, lifetimes when you were the leaders who called forth your affinity, your friends in righteous service unto me as to what you believed in that lifetime. Always I have been with you and always you have been with me.

Now I would speak with you about awakening to see the world and its happenings in a new light, to see the true meaning of life.

There is joy in life itself: the simple joy of being. Now, your world does not say that to you. Your world says that you must accomplish. You have to get through a pile of work every day. There are deadlines that you have to meet and fulfill.

The world does not say to you to take a deep breath and to feel happy about yourself. But I say unto you, if not now, when? In other words, allow yourself to be joyful, to put the smile on the face, and no matter what is happening around you, to stand in joy of yourself.

No matter how much chaos may be happening around you—and there will be some chaos, because that has been part of the human condition—be able to say, "That is not me. I rise above it," as I did upon the cross. I rose above the worldly power that seemed that they would have the last choice. I allowed myself to rise above it and to know my Christ Self.

You are the Christ essence; otherwise, you would not be here. Take that deeply to heart. What does it mean to be of the Christ essence? It means that truly you are not limited by time or space or by what the brothers and sisters say that you have to do. You are not limited by anything except your own choices, and you are free in every moment to choose anew, as I did.

I went through the crucifixion experience in order to prove that one is not the body. You are not the body. You have created the body in order to express the divine power of Is-ness. You are the creator of the body. Now, I know the bodies scream at you sometimes and say that they are in charge. But, in truth, you are the one who has the choice to take the deep breath and to say, "No, I will abide in peace."

In this moment right now, allow yourself to take a deep breath and to feel the peace that comes with the deep breath. You do not have to pay golden coins for the peace that comes with the deep breath. It is a divine gift that you give yourself. The very first thing that you have done when you took the incarnation was to take the deep breath. Some of you saw the great power with that deep breath, and you allowed the vocalization to be quite powerful. Some of you came a little more quietly, but the very first thing that you do in a human incarnation is to breathe.

Part of the essence of humanhood is to breathe. With the deep breath you allow yourself to abide for a moment in peace. Allow yourself to take another deep breath, just an easy breath, just to feel the peace that comes with it, because there is healing that comes with peace. For a moment or so you can set aside all of the worries. You can set aside all of the demands of the world.

Any time you feel that the world is too much with you, allow yourself the deep breath. There were times in my lifetime that I took myself away from the multitudes, even away from the disciples, and communed with the Father with the breathing. I allowed myself to return again to the place of peace, the place where you receive divine guidance.

Even in the Garden of Gethsemane I took myself apart from the disciples and I prayed; I did the deep breathing, and I listened. There was silence, and there was peace about the morrow. And with the peace I knew that I had to go forward. I also knew that I was not going to be alone on the next day with all of the happenings that I had intuited; I knew the probabilities.

I had been speaking a truth that was necessary—and still is necessary in this day and time—of the divinity of each and every one of the brothers and sisters and how they are not—and you are not—under the thumb of government and leaders and of situations; that you are Love expressing, creating.

The idea that you are loved with an everlasting Love and that you are free to create any and all dimensions of your life did not go along with what was being taught in the Temple. The ones who were the rulers at that time, and thought they had the power, decided that this rabble rouser needed to be silenced. So I knew the probability of what was going to be happening on the next day.

And in the silence of the deep breath and in the peace, I knew my strength. I knew my wholeness. Any time when the world is too much with you—and I know that from time to time the world screams at you that you must do such and such or be such and such—allow yourself the deep breath first of all. It is the first step. It is a powerful step.

Then listen in that peace. Listen for guidance. If no guidance comes, breathe again. Keep on breathing. It is a good thing to do for the body; it keeps the body going. (Smile) And listen. Abide in the peace of that breath. That is the simplest of all things that you can do, and it allows you to touch the divinity of you. Breathe and feel the peace.

If you remember nothing else from this message, remember my suggestion that you take a deep breath, over and over if necessary, and abide in peace, because there you will connect with the divinity of you, with the true power of you. The peace that you feel is your power.

Others can taunt you, others can judge you, but they cannot destroy your peace. Only you can destroy your peace, and only you can bring it in with the deep breath. So I highly suggest that you allow yourself, as often as you remember, to abide in peace and to listen, because there are many unseen ones, angels you will call them, loved ones perhaps who have laid down the body, who want to let you know how much you are loved.

Perhaps there were ones of the loved ones who did not know how to love you when you were small, and perhaps they passed on the generational teaching that to be hard with you was to make you strong. All it did was to challenge your spirit and sometimes bring you down a bit. Now that they have laid down the body, they see things differently and they want to tell you how much you are loved.

They want to tell you that they understand now that it was an agreement that you would come together and to be born into a certain family, that there was agreement that you would serve each other. And now they understand that the greatest power of all is not the abusive, hard power, but the greatest power of all is love.

They love you, and they wait to tell you. Sometimes you are so busy and you are listening to other voices—the voices of the world—and they cannot get through. But as you take the deep breath, and as you abide in peace, you will receive a knowing, a knowing from your guardian angel, a knowing from a loved one, a knowing from your inner self, your higher Self, that will guide you and see you through whatever is going to be in the next moment or the next day, the same as the strength I received on the evening in the Garden of Gethsemane.

I knew that I was not going to be alone. I knew that I was being guided to make demonstration that the body is not who you are. You are the Energy; you are the spirit that activates the body. You are the creator of the body.

So when you take the deep breath and you abide in peace, there is healing that comes, a healing peace that allows you to know that truly you have chosen rightly to be in this incarnation, whether or not your separated ego says you are doing okay or not. Separated ego often will say unto you that you are making wrong choices, that you *should* do this or you should *not* do that.

That is separated ego which is separated from its Source and thinks that it has power, the power of the world. But separated ego is only a creation that you have created to be a companion in this journey of human life. It will speak to you of judgment, it will speak to you of pain, it will speak to you of worry, but it is not who you are.

You are the I AM Ego that has been forever, and after the purpose of time has been fulfilled—because there will not always be time—after the purpose of time has been fulfilled, you will still be the Is-ness of divine Love. So allow yourself the simplicity of going within to the place of peace and call upon me. Always I will answer.

Now, in order to know my answer, you have to listen. You may ask of me in that place of peace, "What should I do? What is my next step? Am I worthy?" And sometimes when I answer you, you are off doing something else that the world has said must be done by three o'clock in the afternoon or whatever time is designated.

Listen. Take the deep breath. Abide in peace. Call upon me. And listen. Always I am with you. There is no place that you can be that I am not. If you descend into the depths of hell, the deepest place of worry and doubt, there I am with you. If you ascend into the heavens and you feel the joy of living, there I am with you in that joy. And I will tell you, joy and trust are good places to abide.

The other suggestion I make unto you—hear me well—is to laugh with me, tell me a funny, a joke. No matter what you are going through, allow yourself to step out of it for a moment or so and to see the humor, the ridiculousness of whatever is going on; to look for the humor in any situation and allow yourself to laugh.

Because truly, even as you go through this lifetime and you feel the heaviness from time to time of this lifetime, know that you have lived many other lifetimes and know that if you choose, you may have another lifetime, either here on holy Mother Earth or any of the other most wonderful planetary bodies that you are beginning to acknowledge and beginning to know about.

Any incarnation, whatever form it may take, is a choice. You always choose where you will go. You choose who you will be with. It is a choice. There is no great master directing where you have to go. There is no great master, no great referee in heaven who says you have to incarnate 89 more times before you will be qualified to be an angel. Already you are the angel in human form. There is no master who has more power than you have.

Every moment is open to improv. That is how powerful you are. Every moment is open to choice. Now, there are ones who can look at probabilities and they can say, "Based on what has been past history, there is a probability that X is going to happen." But it is only a probability, and you are the one who chooses whether it comes into your reality or not.

Never do you choose wrongly. You make choices. Every moment you make choices in order to create and in order to play with your creations; not to suffer the slings and arrows of the world; not to suffer.

I did not suffer on the cross. That has been a story handed down to you so that you would feel guilty, that somehow you were part of a collective consciousness a long time ago that wanted to and had the power to make me suffer. But I did not suffer. I looked upon the world, as I looked upon Jerusalem, and there was a sorrow that I felt because brothers and sisters did not yet recognize the power of love and harmony.

You look out upon your world and there is a bit of sorrow that you feel, perhaps, that the brothers and sisters do not yet understand how to live in peace and in harmony. But how are they going to know that unless you example it for them, unless you live in peace with yourself? And from you then it spreads to others.

There is a strong possibility that there will be a lot of drama happening in the days to come. As you are able see it as drama, knowing that the Awakening will be served by the drama, and being able to be the divine Beholder of all and you do it with a smile on your face, you teach others that they have a choice. It is powerful for them to know that they have a choice, that they too can smile in the midst of a beating, whether it be emotional or physical. Humanness does not like abuse. It feels pain. But if you can rise above the pain and the abuse and the judgment, if you can smile at it even in the face of what looks horrendous, you change the vibration of the collective consciousness. That is how powerful you are.

That is what I did. I looked upon the soldier who was pounding the big spikes into my hands. And they were not tiny little nails. They were big spikes to hold me on the cross. I looked into the eyes of the one who was doing his job—because it was his job—and I looked upon him as brother to brother. I loved him, as I do now—he has reincarnated and he has followed me throughout lifetimes—because truly we are joined in the Is-ness of divinity.

I looked with love, and in that moment he was changed because I could see him in love just doing his job. If you are in a position of employment or a place where you are being crucified, look upon it with love, and it will change before your very eyes. Allow yourself the deep breath that brings the peace to you. In that space of peace there is great power to see anew and to choose anew.

We have often spoken of the great Love which allows you to be, and to be all that you choose to be. You are the expression of the one Source, the Creator. You have chosen that you will be here in this time and that you will usher in a new way of looking at everything, because you will smile; again, a very simple thing to do; not always easy if someone is pounding on you or if it feels like the employer is pounding on you; but to smile as if you know an inner secret, because you do.

You know that you are not of the world. The world is of your making, and you can change it moment by moment.

You are not the body. You use it, but it is not your master. The friends, coworkers, acquaintances all have their own perspective of things, and that perspective may or may not resonate with you. It does not have to, because their journey of awakening is different from yours.

Their other lifetimes and their experiences are different from what you have had. What they have brought with them into this lifetime is different from what you have brought into this lifetime. So you cannot judge another one's journey, and they cannot judge your journey. They may try. Oftentimes friends and colleagues will judge, but how can they judge when they have not walked in your sandals? They cannot know what you have experienced either in this lifetime or in other lifetimes, so they judge imperfectly.

You allow them to say what they are going to say, and then you smile. And they wonder, "How can they smile when I have just said that they are the most uninformed, misread, un-understanding person who ever walked the face of the Earth? How can they smile? And they even look like they love me, and I have just used a lot of four-letter words. How can they smile at me?"

Easy, because you know Who and What they are at the soul level. It may not be what they are acting, but in their essence, the deepest part of them, their true being, they are the Christ, and you recognize the Christ and you love the Christ. You may not love the actions or the choices that they make, but you love their being, and you can smile in the midst of whatever is coming down.

You are ready for the peace that the world does not know, the peace that passes the understanding of the world. You can go to your inner Self, the place of peace and silence within, and know that always you will be taken care of. I guarantee it.

No matter what you face, you will be taken care of and you will come through it healed, whole, and knowing your divinity; not as the world defines everything, but as your divinity defines it.

You have known, in other lifetimes, the process that has led to this now moment. You have been preparing for the consciousness of this time all other lifetimes, from the moment you descended into density, from the moment you began to forget Who you are, from the moment you decided you would identify with your creations rather than identify with the creative Source that you Are.

You started a process which is now coming to fruition. It is a process of Light, more and more Light coming into your experience, more and more Light coming into your body, more and more Light coming into your relationships, more and more Light coming into your heart, to the place where you walk every day with the smile on the face, because you know Who you are and it feels good.

I know That Which you are. I honor That Which you are. I love That Which you are, always and forever.

So be it.

MOVING INTO LIGHT CONSCIOUSNESS

I would speak with you now about moving into Light consciousness, the expanded consciousness where you take yourself lightly. I would ask of you, do you live your life lightly or heavily? For the most part? Most likely, you find that some of the time you live your life lightly. Other times there are issues that really get to you. The voice of the world tells you that life is a struggle. It is full of challenge. And no matter how you come up over one challenge and another, there will always be another obstacle on the horizon for you.

However, as you will use a bit of discipline to choose to look upon things lightly, it gets easier to see the Light in every occurrence. And the converse of that is true: as you focus on what is wrong in life, then there seems to be more and more wrong. You have a saying in your world, "Misery likes company." Misery will attract its own, but lightness also attracts its own.

In Truth, you and the brothers and sisters—the collective consciousness—are moving into Light consciousness. Also, our holy Mother Earth is evolving, making changes as the Light being which She is.

Now, I know that for many of the brothers and sisters it is difficult to see any Light around the Earth. The Earth is just something that they walk on, drive on, pave over so that they can have more roads and more dwelling places and structures upon it. And there is not much thought that there could be Light within and around our holy Mother, the Earth, but there is because She is Light coalesced into form, the same as your body. A bigger form, but it is Light and there is consciousness, intelligence; otherwise, there would not be the coalescence into form. There has been a conscious choice of the Intelligence—and I use that with a capital "I"—to bring together a certain form dense enough that humanoids can walk on it and have no care, no thought for it, for the most part.

But the Earth is also a consciousness and is also evolving, allowing more and more of the Light to be acknowledged, radiated into what you would call outer space. I will call it inner space because it is all within the Mind of God and the Mind of the One. And there is a certain evolution, even an acceleration of evolution, which is well in process. There is an acceleration within your own individual consciousness and there is an acceleration of the evolution of Light awareness within and around the Earth. You are being witness to the Earth changes and changing weather patterns. Much is shifting, sometimes dramatically.

Now, whenever you have an evolutionary process going on—and it is always going on, for the holy Child, the one Mind, being creative, is forever ongoing and creating and expanding—you have an evolution of creation; hence, the Earth changes.

There continues to be an evolution within your sandbox, this reality, which has said for a long time, "I have edges around my sandbox to keep my sand in." Now, even in this sandbox there is an evolution in thinking, in willingness, in allowance to entertain the possibility, the probability and the reality that the edges are not so rigid as has been thought in previous times. There is a new contemplation of expandability, fluidity, Light. And when I speak of Light, I do not mean light in the physical sense, although you will, in Truth, see that, too. But I speak of Light as Intelligence.

So, as you are moving into Light consciousness, you will be moving into more awareness of the divine Intelligence of you, the expandedness of you. And our holy Mother, the Earth, is also making this shift into more Light consciousness.

Now, as there is evolution, there are changes which happen as you leave the old thinking behind. And as there is more Light, the Light will show up, first of all, any resistance to it. You are seeing now much resistance to change, to new thinking. Ones are wanting to hold on to old patterns of thinking, old belief systems because they are familiar. New thinking brings about changes, and the ego which believes itself to be separate from its Source does not trust change. So you are seeing much divisiveness between brother and brother, sister and sister, as the old ways of belief are being challenged. Old ways, while they may not be judged to be the best, are at least familiar.

You know this in your own individual life, where old thinking has perhaps not been the harbinger of peace, but at least it was familiar. You have seen some shadows in this lifetime, some issues, as the light of new thinking has shown up areas where there could be change. And then you have set about dealing with the shadows, the issues, with the light of your own intelligence—which is not separate from the One Intelligence—and you have allowed a transformation to take place with those issues.

You have been called upon and volunteered to be the Light consciousness which knows that all is in the divine order of the atonement: the realization of at-One-ment. You have, in truth, before this incarnation, volunteered to be what you see as a certain storage place, a battery, of peace. Now, I hear you saying, "Well, Jeshua, I don't know if I'm much of a battery for peace, because I sure have the ups and downs in my life and I don't always feel peaceful." But, in truth, you as an individual soul, and also as part of a vaster soul group, have volunteered to be the presence of peace while changes are happening.

I say this unto you because I wish to awaken within you the remembrance of what you volunteered for and to reassure you that you volunteered because you know at a very deep level of consciousness that you are the stream, the flow of peace, of Light, of divine Intelligence.

For, as you will see changes on the surface of our holy Mother, the Earth, the physical changes, you will also see changes happening which have been brewing for a while between brother and brother, sister and sister, to the place of boiling point. There are going to be and have been uprisings, for there has been a growing frustration. Breathe peace into those uprisings, whether they be in your area as coworkers who do not agree with each other or as uprising at a farther distance as you measure geography. Breathe peace, and know that truly the holy Child is arising as the phoenix out of every conflagration, every seeming problem. The divinity has to come to a place of remembrance and reawakening.

You have decreed before there was descent into density, before there was the descent into knowing creation from the inside out, that there would be the phoenix of you arising out of the ashes, so you will see ashes. Some of the ashes may be rather large, but they do not have to be: and that is where you come in again.

You are the one who volunteered to be the presence of peace during this time of awakening. You are the one who has said, "I am the adventurer. I have been through multitudinous adventures, and I know myself to be eternal because

I have come through multitudinous adventures. I know that I will prevail." There is a knowing deep within you of Light consciousness.

Know you that this is not the first lifetime you have volunteered to do this. However, this lifetime it is going to be easier for you than some other lifetimes, because you have also gone through an evolutionary process of awakening within your own belief system, as you see your individual history. This lifetime will not require of you what you have given in some other lifetimes, for in other lifetimes you have released the body in most sacrificial terms. That will not be asked of you in this lifetime. But you have volunteered to be the presence of peace, to be the presence of Light consciousness. I am impressing that upon you.

You have set a certain time schedule—you collectively—and you are now at a point where—how do you put this?—the push has come to shove.

Now, having said all of this, it is not to instill fear. In truth, you will find that one day will be pretty much the same as another day because you have been gradually leading up to the awakening. My message to you is remember what you have volunteered to do: to be the presence of peace, to live in Light and to take yourself lightly—and others as well, as often as is possible.

Remember that you are eternal. Remember that you have decreed that there will be an evolutionary process of the phoenix arising. Remember that you are so loved that you are the presence of love.

That is where I abide all of the time and outside of time, for you see, I take myself lightly. There are many in your world who take me heavily, many who, when my name is mentioned, recoil because of previous teaching, because of previous heaviness. Give them another name: tell them that your companion is Fred, or whatever. There has been, down through what you see as the lineage of time, a certain belief system which has grown up about me and about what I taught. A seriousness. And yet my message was always one of simplicity, of love, of Oneness with the Father.

Now, beloved one, I wish for you joy. I wish for you celebration and freedom. I wish for you to play as the child. To go as the child. To remember the innocence of the Child. I wish for you peace and love, harmony, enthusiasm. I wish for you revelation and answers to all of the questions, and I wish for you the knowing of the Light consciousness.

I meet you there.

So be it.

THE OUT-OF-BODY EXPERIENCE

Beloved one, we have spoken often about the importance of the breath. We have suggested that you take the deep breath quite often during the day to allow yourself to ascend unto the place of Beholder to just watch what you are doing, what you are thinking, what the other ones who are in conversation with you are thinking, how they are feeling.

It will be most instructive to you and a bit amusing, because you may be feeling that what you are speaking of is the most important thing, and you are putting it forth to the other one, and the other one is not especially hearing you. They are rehearsing what they are going to say back to you when you stop talking.

So it behooves you not to take your hologram and yourself too seriously; in other words, allow yourself to be the Beholder and to watch the interaction in the hologram, how the interaction is happening, and to have a sense of humor about it.

Now, I know that from time to time you get a little bit emotional about something that is going on and you get into old patterns of thinking. You put on the judge's robes, as you have called them, and you get into judgment, at least for a moment or so until you catch yourself and you say, "Okay, I've put on the judge's robes again; I'm into judging, and I really do not know the whole of the hologram. I don't know what is going on with the other person, so I really can't judge unless I have been and am in their sandals, walking in their sandals and understanding where they are coming from."

But as you allow yourself to be in the place of Beholder, you will see more and more of yourself; in other words, there is nothing outside of you. Everything that you see comes from a place of resonance within yourself, either as you will have experienced it *this* lifetime or from previous lifetimes or from some reading that you have done. Perhaps it comes from some of the moving dramas you have watched when you feel you are living that life in what would be the two hours of your movie.

You get right into it, and it is as if you are experiencing that in your lifetime very quickly. That is why you have brought forth the moving dramas: so that you can review, re-look at the lifetimes you have had. Sometimes when you are watching one of the moving dramas, you relate to what is going on in that drama and you say, "I know how that feels. How are they going to get out of that situation?"

And you may be right on the edge of the chair, or perhaps taking a deep breath and sitting back and saying, "I know that they're going to work through this." Well, yes, you have. So when you watch the moving dramas, allow yourself to recognize that *you* have played those parts. You have been in situations, sometimes very scary situations which you have been very happy to leave.

But it is all within you. There is nothing outside of you. The great news about that is, the vastness of what ***is*** you and what you can imagine has a place of relatedness within you, because if you can imagine it, you have already been there. So when you see situations and you get caught up in either the moving drama or a book that you are reading or even in a coworker's drama that they are telling you about, allow yourself the deep breath and go to the place of Beholder and watch it as it would be a hologram right in front of you, and see your place in it. See how you are affecting the interchange that is going on. Even as you have the emotions that are aroused, you are in those moments very much in that drama. You would say, "Well, it's just on the big screen and I'm just sitting watching it," but where does all of the emotion, and even the story, come from?

"Oh well, somebody scripted it, somebody I don't even know; their name is up on the big screen." Yes and no. You share with them the authorship of it, because if you were not watching it, it would not be happening.

Everything is within you. That is why we have spoken previously about expanding your hologram, expanding what you believe your reality to be: watching it as a hologram in front of you and then expanding it to know that there is much more, taking the hologram back as far as you can imagine, back to the Big Bang and before that.

You play with ideas; exciting ideas. "How would it feel to be able to change the world? Where would I start? How? Well, I'd have to gather a group of friends around me and probably ones who have a lot of the golden coins so that we could effect change."

But if everything is within you, you really do not need anyone else. "Oh, but yes, I do. I can't do it on my own. I'm supposed to go and talk to Pharaoh? I wouldn't know what to say." But the burning bush said, "Go. Talk to Pharaoh. And you will be told what to say."

You will be told the next step, because everything that you think about, everything that you dream about that you want to do is possible if you will take the first step. Everything. It has to be possible, because you are the extension of the creative Principle and you are creating your hologram, your reality as you go along—lowercase "r".

It is your Reality—capital "R"—which allows you to think that you are powerless; that, "Well, I can do a little bit of good, and if somebody is hurting, I can give them an encouraging word, but I can't really change the world."

Yes, you can. You can change your world. That is how powerful you are. You make your world every moment. As you change your world, you may find that your hologram has expanded to take in others. Now, in truth, there are not others. There's only One of us. But you have made a reality that believes in separation, that believes in bodies and in duality and the gradations between good and not so good. But if you have made that—and I assure you that you have—you can change it.

Why not? You have already done a miracle in providing yourself with a body and saying that it extends only so far, even if you take in the aura of it. Or if you do not, it only extends to the edge of the skin. It is a miracle in itself, and you do it moment by moment by moment so that it seems to be a continuum.

The out-of-body experience is something that you can have without deceasing the body. Let's do a bit of what you call a meditation. Allow yourself to be comfortable and to soften the eyes a bit. Allow yourself to breathe easily, and know that the body is comfortable and you do not have to worry about it. It is going to take care of itself.

Now feel yourself in your mind's eye looking down on the body. Just how does it look on the chair? Does it look comfortable? If you feel like you have to wiggle the toes or move around a bit, that is okay. How does the top of the head look? How do the shoulders look? What shirt/jacket do you have on? How does it look?

How much light is in the room? Is there a growing light? How does it feel to look down upon yourself in the light?

There is one who is calling to you, one whom you love very much, and they are standing right next to you above the body, looking down at the body the same as you are. There is one standing right next to you, by your left elbow and smiling, and their love encompasses you. Their love flows to you and through you, and there is a responding love that flows back from you to them, and there is a feeling of peace, a feeling of security.

Ask of them, "What would you tell me? What is most important that I should know now? I have been thinking about…" whatever you have been thinking about. "What would you tell me? Is there something that I need to do? Is there something I need to just let go of? Is there something that is already in process?"

And you feel at peace. You feel transported out of the body, above the body. You still have connection to the body, but you are not the body. The loved one who stands next to you is allowing you to see that you are love, and you feel your love expanding.

Then you look up and you see the stars. You see the heavens with the glittering lights of stars. There is one that goes very fast, and you know it to be alive with brothers and sisters whom you have known. And the loved one who stands at your elbow nods, "Yes, those are ones you have known and will come to know again." The stars are your friends, and your friends are in the stars.

All is you. Allow yourself to feel expansive, secure, floating, free, alive, and yet not having to care. And the loved one who stands at your elbow whispers in your ear a message only for you, a message for you. There is a sense of peace and calm that you know you will always feel and take with you.

And then when the message is finished, the one who loves you and is standing by your elbow whispers to you that it is time for you to return to the focus of the body, but that they will always be at your elbow, and they will always be accessible to you.

And so, taking a deep breath, allow the focus of your attention to return to the body, once more sitting on the chair. And when it is easy, focus your eyes and you will find yourself right where you have always been.

You can go to that place any time you want to. All it requires is that you take a deep breath and release the very strong focus you have on the body, the identification with the body. The body will always serve you. It will always be your servant. But more and more, as you are expanding your understanding of reality, you are going to find yourself above the body, looking from the place of Beholder, finding your answers in the space that is not attached to the body, in the divinity that is the Reality—capital "R"—of you.

That knowing is what I have been leading you to all of these months and years, where we have talked about various aspects of being. We have often been speaking of reality—lowercase "r"—and the hologram, and you have wondered, "Why is he still talking about the hologram? It's a great idea, but I can't see it having import in my life, and I don't know why he keeps coming back to the hologram."

I come back to it because it is the truth of what you are living, and if it is a hologram and you are creating the hologram right in front of you and all around you, you can change it. That is my gospel. That is my good news to you. And one of these days it is going to sink in to the place where you are going to say, "Hey, I can make changes. I can change everything and anything that I want to change. I am not at the mercy of anybody else's dictates," because truly there is not anyone separate from you.

"And if I'm making all of these rules and regulations and saying how weak I am and how these limitations have to affect me, well, I've gone off the track of remembering Who I am; not only Who I am, but What I am."

And I say unto you very strongly, **in this lifetime *yet*, you will know Who and What you are.** You will ***know*** it in this lifetime.

Wake up and know that you are your own teacher. Wake up and know that you are your own Christ, the Christed One, all-powerful to change everything into love. That is how powerful you are.

If you want love, I give it to you. It is yours, free. If you want health, I give it to you. If you want many years to enjoy this lifetime, I give it to you; it is yours. The only small catch is, you have to accept it. If you want a better world, I give it to you, because there is no separation. Everything that you recognize and acknowledge in your world comes from you.

"Well, that's hard to imagine. You mean I'm creating all of those wars that I hear about in my news media? You mean I'm creating all of those dis-eases? You mean I'm the one who is creating the bad guys? Why would I do something like that? I wouldn't do that, Jeshua. I wouldn't do that."

You have, because you like to play with drama. You like the adrenaline rush. You like the challenge. You have accepted generational teaching about how the world is, and you have developed a belief in separation that says that there can be other than you, other than good. But now you are crying out, literally crying out—I hear you—for a better world.

Allow yourself to come out of the body, to rise above the body, and to imagine that which would be a better world, and know that when you come back into the body, the world will be changed because *you* will be changed. It is as simple as that.

If you hold onto the old way of thinking, it is separated ego only that keeps you from knowing the Oneness, the Allness, the Powerfulness of the Christ of you. Now, that is putting it pretty straight. It is only separated ego that wants to be attended to.

Allow yourself to ascend into the I Am Ego. It will not take you from knowing what is going on around you. You will still be aware of the world and what is going on around you, but you will have a different perspective, a different view of everything that is happening, and you will understand why the things that you have perceived to be happening have been perceived.

Part of the journey, part of the exquisite creativity of the one divine extension—I will not call you Child, because that implies separation—is to know how great you are; not great in the sense of the world's adulation, but great as the one divine extension of the creative Principle; that is how great you are. No one in a long, long time has told you that, but I tell it to you truly. You are powerful. You are All. Everything that you would imagine is within you. The kingdom of Heaven is within you. And so is the kingdom of Hell.

Furthermore, there is no judgment. If you want to stay in the place that sees drama, that sees challenge, there is no judgment as to how long or how many lifetimes you want to go over the same scripting. There is no judgment. But if you want to change—and I know that you are calling out for at least a little bit of change—you can do it.

I will be with you. I will add my power, which is the same as your power, to yours, and together, as you still understand some separation, we are powerful. And then you will come to know that I am not outside of you.

"Oh, my goodness, you mean that the one that I have worshipped and who has been speaking to me for a good two thousand years one way or another is within me?"

I am. I abide within you. Make a loving place for me. Put your arms around me, within yourself. What you end up doing is hugging yourself; great. Go on; put your arms around me. Thank you. It feels kind of good. Any time you want to be hugged, you want to hug me, you can do it. And if you have no arms—as there are ones who do not have arms—imagine.

That is why you built into this reality the gift of imagination, so that you could walk out of this reality once in a while and imagine how it would feel to live a different kind of life.

Never have I left you. If we are One—and I assure you that we are—and if I am always with you, I cannot abandon you. If you descend into the depths of hell—and you have been there; you have struggled; you have cried; you have screamed; you have pounded, and you felt like you were in hell—I am there with you.

If you ascend into the heavens and you feel like you have finally "got it" — "I've got it; I know it now; I feel it"—I am with you there. Always I am with you. Never are you abandoned.

So when you are getting ready to change some of your world, some of your reality, one of the first things you can kick out of that reality is the feeling of separation, of abandonment. Give it a good kick so that it does not come back. I cannot—I would not--but I *cannot* abandon you. I cannot leave you. We are made of the same stuff, the same divinity, so always I walk with you.

Play with being the Beholder. Play with the imagination of being out of body. See how it looks from above. Feel how it feels to be above it. You will not decease the body. You do not have to worry that, "Well, if I go too far, the silver cord is going to be severed and I'll lose the body and they'll take care of it and bury it somewhere and I'll never find it again."

No, that is not going to happen. Allow yourself to play with the imagination, the out-of-body experience, to know that you are more than the body. Allow yourself to feel the power and the peace of the Beholder, and know that always I Am You.

So be it.

CONNECTING WITH YOUR GOD SELF

Beloved one, as we have said, you are the maker of everything in your universe. You are the maker of all of your reality. That is a bit much to grasp, because you have been taught through what seems to be eons of time that you were just a small speck, unworthy to even think of yourself as being from the divine, unworthy to know even a name to call yourself. Can you imagine there was a time when you were not allowed and not thought to be worthy to even have a name?

Now you have come into this lifetime and you have sometimes a great string of names, all of them descriptive of you. For you gather to yourself as a history a lineage of names, and they describe who you are, where you have come from, who supposedly the genealogical parents/ancestors are/have been, what your professional title may be, etc.

So you feel that you have a long, long history—and you do. It extends even farther back than what you can imagine. It goes back to the place where you knew yourself to Be, just to be divine energy forever flowing, forever creating, forever imagining whatever you wanted to imagine.

You stand now in a place, a choice-point, where truly you have choices and you want to choose well. You have said, "I've played this scenario long enough. I have played being unworthy. I have played being the victim. I have played being the victor. I have played all of the different scenarios that I can think of. Now I want to know peace. I want to know worthiness. I want to know ease of being. I want to know the love of others who gather round and feel my love flowing out towards them. I want to feel in the midst of love."

You are going to allow yourself to dream, "How can this come about? How can this be? How can I make the dream a reality—lowercase 'r'—and then how can I know that it truly comes from my Reality—capital 'R'?" You are beginning to feel possibilities. They seem yet beyond your grasp. They are just beyond the fingertips. But there are choices. There is a reality, a reality that fulfills what you are seeking deep within yourself.

As some of the time goes by, you are going to make the move, the steps to bring this into your conscious reality; not just a dream, but you are going to make it manifest. Allow yourself a moment right now to ask of yourself, "What is my deepest desire? What would I like to see made manifest? What in my life would I do, experience, if I could?"

At first you will have ideas and the ego will say, "Well, that's just an idea, a dream." But the more you think about it and you look at possibilities as to what would be the first step to making this manifest, you see that you *can* take a step to make it a reality. You *can* connect with the power that you are—not power that you have, but power that you are—and bring together that which you truly desire at a very deep level.

You can do this. It is time. You have in your reality a belief, a very deep-seated belief in process, in time, that everything has a beginning, a middle which is probably quite long, and then an achievement of the goal, whatever the goal may be. And when you get to the goal, you find that there can be a refinement of the goal. There can be more, because then you have a new perspective, and then you move on to making some more changes.

Nothing is ever set in concrete. I have said to you many times that it is most wonderful what you do with the improvisation. I watch you as you think you are stuck in something. "I really have to do it this way. This is what the world tells me it has to be." And then you make some improv. You change in a moment.

You are going to be making some changes that even now seem to be impossible. You are going to say, "But I have to leave behind some of the things that I have thought were important." Well, if they are that important to you, you are going to bring them along with you into the new reality. If they do not come into the new reality with you, they were never that important. They served their place for a time, and then you are a new person. You get to change.

Separated ego may say, "But I don't really want to change, because at least the suffering that I do, I know it and it is familiar. It hurts, but I know it." But I say unto you, you do not have to keep your hologram in limitation. Your hologram, your reality, the illusion of reality can be anything that you want it to be, and it can be any time that you want it to be.

Allow yourself to take all of the limitations off of the illusion of this reality, and know that truly you can walk out into what seems to be thin air and you will still be supported. You have to be, because you are the one creating. So take that step into what seems to be thin air. Put on the earmuffs so that you do not hear separated ego. Allow the I Am Ego of you to flourish.

This is the time now. There is no other time that you need to wait for. It will seem to separated ego that you are doing an upheaval, and you are. So when separated ego starts talking to you and says you cannot do this, put the earmuffs on. Allow yourself to move forward and to say, "Yes, this is what I want to do. This is where I want to go. This is what I feel guided to do." It may not seem logical. It may not even seem possible. But if you want something truly at the soul level and it is like life itself to you, then this is the time to move forward on it. There will never be a better time. If not now, when? What are you waiting for? If there is a desire deep within your soul, listen to it. Act on it. Allow it to come forth, even if it means that you have to make big, big, changes. *Everything* is possible.

All you have to do is, first of all, take the deep breath. Second of all, get clear about what your soul is really longing for and what it would look like, and then to ask, "What is the first step?" You do not have to know all of the steps. That may be where separated ego runs in and says, "But it's too much, master. I can't handle all of that." Of course not; you only have to handle the first step, and then the second step will be made clear to you.

"Oh, but I can't do that." Why not? You have made other big changes in your life, even if you did not know what was going to be happening. As you look back on this lifetime, you can see that you were guided by your higher Self, by your soul. You were guided. Even though you might not have known it, there was a drawing forth from the soul level for you to be making manifest that which you truly desired.

Long enough have you waited. Long enough have you put it aside because you thought it was not possible. Long enough you have found reasons why you could not allow the soul's desire to become manifest. Now you connect with the God Self of you, and from the God Self of you, all things are possible.

I know. I faced in my lifetime, the lifetime that is so famous, times when things seemed to be quite impossible. And I questioned. And yet there was a knowing from the soul level to do, to go places, to speak. "Who am I," I said, "to speak that which I know? I'll speak it to a few people. I'll collect a few disciples unto myself and I'll teach a small group," such as the ones that I had been in and had learned from—the master teachers that I studied with. "I'll have a small group of ones and I will share that which the masters have shared with me. I will share with a small group."

Well, that was not the soul purpose—s-o-u-l; s-o-l-e—purpose. And I found more and more people hungering to know their freedom, their joy; wanting to know that which I knew—first, at a mental level…you see, it did not all come right away. There was a period of testing out. There was a period of trying, trusting, moving forward, even until the crucifixion and the resurrection.

Did I know that I could resurrect the body? Mentally I knew I could. But in truth—lowercase "t"—I was not quite sure. But there was a direction from the soul, as you have had in this lifetime. And the best way to know the soul direction, what it is calling out to you to do, is to look back on this lifetime and to see how you have been guided; how you have made choices when you did not even know you were making a choice. But you chose, and it has brought you here to this point.

You have a deep yearning at the soul level, and there are times when you are going to question, "Is this truly from my soul?" Well, if it does not seem to make sense, it is probably from your soul, because separated ego likes everything to make sense. And if reasons come up that say, "Well, you had better not make that choice," with a fear-based feeling, then you will know that that comes from separated ego, which has held you for a while until there was enough energy to burst forth.

It does not have to be difficult. The only time it is difficult is when you believe it has to be difficult in order to prove something to yourself or perhaps to others. That is the only time when it seems to be difficult. The rest of the time you go according to what you feel brings you joy.

You may have to sit with yourself for a while, and you may have to go deep within yourself to find what brings you joy. There is always a chance to go deeper and to feel more joy, to the place where truly you cannot keep the feet upon our holy Mother Earth.

This is the lifetime when you are awakening. You have prayed other lifetimes that you would know more of your-Self—capital "S"—that you would know more of what everything meant and why you were experiencing what you were experiencing. This lifetime then has come so that you can consciously know that you are a master, so that you can consciously know that you create; that you put together all of the pieces even though it may seem at the time that the pieces are coming together for different reasons—maybe not even for the highest reasons. And yet when you look back, you will see that the choices *were* for the highest and best.

A lot of times when you are sleeping—and I do not mean in the nighttime sleeping, but a lot of times when you are going about your business focusing upon the worldly issues and what needs to be done--the soul of you is working, orchestrating the next step, and you may not consciously...you probably *are* not conscious of what is going on, but you make the choices directed by the God Self of you or the soul of you, the soul that truly wants to awaken.

You are connected to every brother and sister. There is no separation—as we have spoken many, many times. You know truly what the other one is feeling and thinking when you want to tune in and when you want to be at One with them. You have a connection that goes back eons of time, as you measure time in this Earthly realm. You have a connection that goes back to before time.

You know truly what it feels like to be free. You ask, "I know what it feels to be free? I thought I had responsibilities. I thought there were things I had to do. I thought everything in life was in certain stages, and I had to fulfill certain stages."

Yes and no. You have come through the stages, but there is a higher purpose, and the higher purpose is to awaken to the place of knowing the God Self of you, the creativity of you, the Oneness of you, the laughter, the joy, the communion of One. That is truly what you want to feel: the communion, the common union of One.

You want to feel that whatever you would be experiencing, you could speak truthfully to another one; not have to couch it in certain language; not have to find the right words, feel the right emotions, but just to be truthful; to be able to lay it all out there and say, "This is who I am; this is what I'm feeling—lowercase 'w'. This is who I am. This is Who I would like to be—capital 'W'. This is Who—capital 'W'—I Am. I can let you see that. There are times when I question if I'm going to open my eyes the next day, or whether it's worth opening my eyes the next day. There are times when I feel abandoned, unsupported, unloved, unworthy. There are times when I don't know just how precious I am."

You have felt this, and you have hidden it from others because you did not want them to reinforce your feelings of unworthiness, so you have hidden it from others and you have tried to hide it from yourself. But all the time it was right out there in vibratory energy for everyone to see and to feel.

What you want to be able to do is to be honest with yourself and honest with other ones and to put it right out there, "This is what I am feeling. Perhaps I shouldn't feel this way, but I do feel this way, and I want to move through it. Will you help me move through it?" And it is okay to be honest in this human experience, to put it right out there and say, "I have tried many different ways, and nothing is satisfying, fulfilling. Nothing takes away the pain, the doubt, the feeling of unworthiness, the feeling of possible abandonment."

We have spoken at other times that all of you who know your connection to me have had very deep reinforcement of the possibility of abandonment when you saw me crucified and when you felt I had left you. When you knew that I had raised Lazarus from the dead, when you knew that I could facilitate healings, when you knew that I had the power to save myself, did I not care enough about you that I would save myself to be with you?

Maybe you said to yourself, "I'm not worth it. Maybe he doesn't want to be with me any longer. He's left me. And if he leaves me, and I know he has the power to stay with me, maybe everybody in my experience, maybe everybody in my whole experience of this lifetime and other lifetimes is going to abandon me because I'm not worth their staying around to help me."

You have carried that at a subconscious level. You have carried the feeling of abandonment, and it is a button that gets pushed easily. You dig yourself very quickly a very deep hole and you think, "Oh, I'm not worthy. I've tried. I've tried my best. See how I've suffered? But I guess I'm not worthy. I guess he/she doesn't care." It goes back to the very deep reinforcement of the belief at the time of the crucifixion.

There were lifetimes before that where there were experiences of abandonment, but that one, for those of you who are close to me, that one went very deep into the psyche, and you have carried it for two thousand years. So where am I now? I am back here with you. Maybe the form is a little bit different, but there are other times when I make my own form and I come and I sit next to you and I talk with you, and you are not quite sure who it is, but it is somebody very friendly and they seem very loving and wise.

I *am* wise, because I *know* That Which you are. And you are wise, because you recognize something in me, and it is the same that abides within you, the God Self, the holy soul of you.

So listen to the deepest yearnings of your heart, of your soul. Get clear as to what you would really like to do, and get busy making it manifest in your experience. Eventually separated ego is going to go off into the wings of the stage and is not going to be needed any more. It will take a while, because separated ego is very used to having a script and running onstage. But after a while there is not going to be any part for separated ego to play and it will stay in the wings, and then finally it will go down and take a seat in the audience and will watch how you go: free, honest, knowing the God Self of you is at play—I will not say work, but in play.

Connect often in quiet times with the breath. Ask of yourself, "Where would I like to be? What would I really like to be doing? What is the first step? Who do I need to talk to?" if that would be the first step. "Who do I have as companion on the journey? Who do I love, and who loves me?"

I will share with you that I love you; always have and always will. Never will I forsake you. Never will I forsake you. Never *can* I forsake you. I love That Which you are. It is That

Which I Am and That Which you are: Love itself; free to express, free to be.

So be it.

THE MASTER SECRET

Down through the ages ones have wanted to know, "Who is God? What is God?" There have been definitions; wise ones have come up with an explanation, a description of God, and yet that is not God. They may describe an aspect of God, but not all of God, for to describe and to define God is to limit It.

God is not a Him or a Her, not even an It as in gender, but an ongoing infinite Energy which is forever expanding from before time began. And after the purpose of time has been fulfilled—believe it or not, there *is* purpose to time—after that purpose has been fulfilled, you as the one Mind, the extension and expression of the one Mind, will keep on expanding, forever asking—not in words, but in the Beingness of energy—"What more can I experience? What more can I create? Where can I express?"

You will keep on creating universes upon universes within universes, physical and spiritual, to the place where you know yourself truly as spirit; not defined by anything; not limited by anything. And yet you have chosen, volunteered to be within this incarnation to take form, to coalesce the Light and the energy that you are, to take form and to walk with other brothers and sisters who yet believe that there has to be a form that they can reach out and touch, a form that they can see, a form that they can speak with.

You have said, "I will go one more time as the Light and the Love of the Father/Mother/God/Goddess/All That Is and I will speak with my brothers and sisters, but more than that, I will *be* with them in the essence of All, in the essence of One."

You are a master. We have spoken of this in other days, in other times. You, because you are a master, before this incarnation and before many other incarnations, have looked upon what was happening in the 3D reality—or sometimes 2D—and you have said, "I will go and bring my Light and my wisdom, as much as will be acceptable, into the experience of the whole." And so, as the master that you are, you have come one more time to serve the awakening of the collective consciousness in the realization of Oneness.

I know that you question this. You say, "Well, if I'm here to serve the awakening and I can see all these issues that are going on, not only in the collective but also in my individual life, how can I be a master? Why, if I am a master, would I ever *choose* to come into such an experience?"

Well, it is because you *are* a master that you did choose, and every day you choose. The overall master secret—and it is not a secret; it is for everyone to know—the master secret is choice, the fact that you have choice. You can choose to abide with the news media and say, "Oh, my God, it is so bad. I don't know how this is ever going to work out. I feel so bad for my brothers and sisters who have to go through the wars and the violence that the news media reports. How is that ever going to lead to an awakening?"

In that moment you have the most wonderful gift: the gift of choice. You can choose to stay in that place where you say how bad it is, or you can say it is completion and demonstration, which truly it is. It is completion, sometimes on the individual level. And many times it is a demonstration for the brothers and sisters to see and to have opportunity to feel empathy, Oneness. Many times ones of the brothers and sisters who are going through great disasters, violence, having all of the family members perhaps giving up the body in most torturous ways, are masters who have volunteered to play that part.

Now, I am not saying that it is easy and I am not saying that they do not suffer, because they do. They know human body experience. They know human emotion. But above and beyond that, the soul of them, the true being of them, is a master who has agreed to play the part so that others can look upon it and see that what is happening is not loving, that it is not of Oneness. It is of division and the un-Truth of separation.

So when you look upon what your news media will bring to you, you have the moment of identification with what is going on. You understand the appearance. You know what is going on. Then you move into the place, as a conscious choice, to thank them for what they are doing to bring you to the place where you can say, "I am complete with it. I want to be in love. I want to greet everyone in love, and I want to have all misunderstandings resolved to the place of understanding Oneness."

When ones will come and bring you an example where there is opportunity to look with human emotion on something, you have the most wonderful master tool of choice. *It is so simple that it is overlooked many times.* It is simplicity itself to choose; not to react, not to judge, not even to see that there would be something to judge; but to be thankful that they are showing the completion of man's/woman's inhumanity to man and woman.

Even on a more personal scale, when you have friends who perhaps see things differently than you do and they bring up the opportunity where you could see divisiveness, you have choice. You can look beyond what they are saying—as you have done—and love them as the being, the true Being that they are. The words do not matter.

You do not realize the great *power* of choice, because separated ego will bring to you the possibility that you could look at this in judgment, saying, "Ah, but it feels so good to stand in judgment because I am superior. I don't know why they are doing what they are doing, so I'm going to judge," and so you do, for a moment or so, and that is okay, because now you know you do not have to stay there. You recognize, "I am standing in a place where I don't have to be. I have the power of choice, of moving out of whatever I have thought the truth—lower case 't'—of this situation is, and I have the power of choice to know the Truth—capital 'T'—of this situation."

Whether it has to do with relationships and the healing thereof or if it has to do with the body and the healing of the body, you have choice as to how you will look upon it—the healing of the planet, the healing of all of the knowledge that you have brought to this incarnation. You have choice.

Now, as I have said, it is simplicity itself; it is so simple that separated ego often downplays it and says, "Ah, yes, but you know, it really feels good to get a little bit of anger going here. I can spend a minute or two with a few choice words." And you can. But the wonderful part that I want you to understand is that you have and you do use the power of choice, whether to abide there or to choose to let it go.

I watch you; I see you as you are letting it go more and more quickly as you are choosing to be in a place that says, "I know love. I feel love. This other is only drama. This other is passing," and it is. "I know the feeling of expansiveness of love, and that is where I choose to abide."

And once you choose to abide in the space of love, you find yourself laughing at the other part of you that has gotten so worked up about something. There is a quotation in another treatise I have authored that says, "I could choose peace instead of this."

But this lifetime you have feelings of judgment. You know human emotions. You know how it feels to have judgment, but you also know how to step out of that space. Your beloved friends, the four-footed ones, your beloved pets do not spend much time in judgment. They can have reaction, but then it passes very quickly.

Everything that you call forth is there because you have called it forth to give you opportunity to choose, to give you opportunity to have the human emotion that is quite well-trained because of many, many lifetimes, and then to have the power of choice to say, "Well, I can stay really angry at this situation," or "I don't think it's worth the energy."

Other ones' judgments, even other ones' facial expressions belong to *them*, and if they have certain facial expression that you could interpret as being rather down-putting, you can laugh. They may wonder what you are laughing at, and you can say, "Well, I just remembered something funny," and you can go on. It changes the whole energy.

The master knows the secret. The secret is choice as to where you will abide. There is no judgment in it. You do not judge yourself for spending a minute, five minutes, five days in a certain place of judgment. And sooner or later—sometimes later—you move out of that space as you have choice and you have power.

That *is* your power, the power of choice, which you have built into this reality. As I have said, it is so simple that it is often overlooked. And we have spoken many times of the power of the smile. When you are toe to toe with someone and you feel really strongly about what he/she said to you, all of a sudden the idea may come, "I don't have to resist this. I can smile." Then you smile, and the other one will ask himself/herself, "What page are they on? They're not on the same page of the script as I am. They must have skipped forward somewhere." And then the energy changes.

Try that. The next time when you have a person who is perhaps *wanting* to give you a hard time, you do not have to take it. You can smile. You can *choose* to be in the space of true communication—common union—which a smile can bring forth. Or perhaps you can *choose* to walk away in love.

You do not have to abide in the place of judgment. You do not have to abide in the place that is unpleasant—even a physical place; you can walk away from it. You can speak your truth, knowing that perhaps another one will not hear it quite the way that you are wanting them to hear it. That does not matter. You smile and you walk away from it.

Many, many lifetimes you have embroiled yourself in drama—heavy, heavy drama—not knowing that there was any other alternative to it. Many lifetimes you have acted according to habitual generational teaching that says if someone throws a stone at you, you have to throw one back at them, whether it be physical or whether it be a mental judgment or a word. But now you know you have the power of choice. You can smile with your bright eyes and move on to something that is more pleasant.

You are a great master who is remembering the simplicity of choice, of the power of choice. You can choose where you want to be. *You can change your world by your choice as to where you will abide. That* is your power.

Abide with me. Laugh often. In the lifetime that is so famous and written about, I laughed often with you, my disciple. For, truly, life *can* be heavy, but it does not have to be. It can be light and taken lightly, and I chose—as I choose in this day and time as I walk with you and as you—I choose to walk lightly and to laugh often, because the drama is just that, and it is passing and it is evolving.

Choose to look on the bright side of things. Choose to look for the light. Choose where you will abide—in light, in love, and with me, always.

So be it.

WHERE DO WE GO FROM HERE?

Beloved one, I have seen you sit with a question, an issue that seems to be quite heavy, and all of a sudden an idea will come to you and you pop up and you do the improv. You go with a third choice that was perhaps not there a few moments ago, or did not seem to be—actually it was, but you did not recognize it—and you do a bit of improv and everything changes, because it has to, because you are the one creating.

You are from the divine one creative Source and you are creative. Wow, are you creative! I have watched you with your creations and I have watched you struggle with some of the visions that you have, and sometimes time seems to be the opponent, and you say, "I'll have to have patience."

You have devised time as a gift in this reality so that you do not get yourself in too much of a muddle right away. If you could instantaneously, in the reality that you are making for yourself, make the choice and be immediately into whatever seems to be the choice, you would oftentimes be jumping from the frying pan into the fire; in other words, maybe into a place where you do not really want to be.

So you have gifted yourself, creative one that you are, the gift of time so that you can contemplate—maybe not for a long time; it does not have to be stretched out, or it can be—and you may see, "Well, if I do such and such, it looks like these are some of the consequences that may come from it. Maybe I want to rethink this."

And as you meditate, as you contemplate, as you rethink, other ideas may come. You do the improv and you come up with a new reality, and sometimes the ones around you will say, "Where is she coming from? Where is he coming from? Where does that idea come from? Why is this happening?"

And you will say, "Because it seems to be a better choice than what I was looking at before. I do not really know where it is going to lead, but I trust that my divine Self knows where it is going to lead and I follow with trust and sometimes with patience." You have also built in, along with time, the gift of patience. Now, you do not use it as often, but it is a gift that you have built in to this reality.

As you are looking at the hologram of what you call your reality, allow yourself to be non-judgmental. Many times separated ego will run onstage and will say, "Well, this hologram, this reality that you are making for yourself, it is really a mess. I don't know how you got into such a mess." That is separated ego which does not recognize the I AM Ego, the true I AM-ness of you. It is a habitual reaction from an old friend with whom you have journeyed many lifetimes.

But now you are coming to the place where you are saying, "Wait a minute. I don't have to judge. Maybe everything I have chosen is in order of leading me to the awakening that I so desire." And it is. Everything that you choose leads you to the next step that leads you to the next step that in time leads you to the place where there is no time.

Later on in this message we will do a meditation which will allow you to come to the place of no time, but right now I am going to speak a little bit longer. All of you who are reading these words are walking into a joyful future as you see linear time. Why? Not because I tell you, but because you have decreed it. You have decreed that you are complete with suffering, with worrying, with fear that someone else might have power over you.

You have decreed at the soul level…and you may say, "Well, I'm not in touch with my soul very much; I believe I do have a soul."That is a good step; that is the first step. "Maybe my soul knows better than I consciously do." And this is true; your soul does know; you do have soul purpose. "Maybe I can walk into that reality." And you can, and you will.

Even in this moment as you read the words, you have moved into a new space of possibility, of probability, a place of hope that says, "I am not confined by anyone else's truth—lowercase "t". I am in a place where I am beginning to understand and take back my power, my divine creative power," which is not a power over anyone else; it is a power of choice, of your own choice. And you can be as happy as you want to be.

"Wow! I never thought about it that way. I can be as happy as I want to be? Hey, maybe I haven't wanted to be." This is true. Oftentimes you have not wanted to be happy. You have wanted the struggle, because at least you were doing something. Or the small ego of you thought you were doing something as you struggled through the "challenges".

So I speak to you of a joyful future; it *is* your divine inheritance to know joy, to be free of world judgment, to be free of small ego, to walk out of time, to walk out of fear, to come to a place where you say, "I'm free," because knowing the Truth of your being will set you free.

The Truth of your being is that you are the divine holy Self—capital "S"—creating every reality that you play in. I remark upon that word, "play", because it *is* a play within a play within a play; sometimes you make it that complex, so that you do not even know that it is a play within a play within a play.

Sometimes within the play within the play you have felt, "Well, he said to me, and he must know because he's my boss—or he's my best friend, he's my older brother, he is my parent, he is my mate—he must know, and he has said this is what it has to be. But, hey, I'm giving him power by saying that because he is in my reality, he knows more than I know. But I am the one giving him power."

He has power in his own reality; you do not deny that. But he does not have power in your reality unless you *believe* he has power in your reality. And you try your hardest—you have done this many, many lifetimes—to give your power away, to say, "Well, I don't want the responsibility of making a wrong choice."

I say unto you, you never make a wrong choice. You make choices and you live with the effects of those choices, but they are all part of your journey. It is the divine journey of awakening, and you have never made a wrong choice. Every choice has led you to a place of being right here, right now, accepting your power for yourself. You are making your reality every moment. That is how powerful you are. And in truth, you cannot give your power away. You can make a reality where it seems you have given your reality to someone else and their beliefs and their prophecies, but in truth, you cannot give your power away, because it is you.

Let that sink in for a moment. Your power is your divine Is-ness, and it is leading you Home. No matter what choices you have made, no matter how often separated ego has screamed at you that you have made a wrong choice, every choice is leading you Home. So be happy in that. Know that truly you are coming Home.

You have desired to be Home once again. You have often said, "This is not my Home. This world is not my Home. I don't feel at home in the world. I don't feel like I fit in. Maybe others fit in, but I don't really feel I fit in. This isn't Home." And you have even asked…as the small one you have asked the parents, "Where's Home?"

And they have said, "Well, you *are* home. This is our dwelling place. You are home." And you said, "No, this isn't Home. It doesn't feel like Home." And that is because you have wanted so much to come Home in your own power and to realize that truly never have you left Home. You cannot. It is within you, and you can never leave Home.

You can *play* with a reality—lowercase "r"—that Home is somewhere else and you have to do all sorts of ritual to find it and to be worthy of finding it. That has been taught to you down through many generations by your "authorities", your religious leaders who have said you have to face in a certain direction, you have to eat certain foods or not eat certain foods; you have to stand on one leg, you have to cross the other leg behind you; you have to hold one nostril closed, etc., all the different rituals that will make you worthy to know your holiness.

And when you have all of those mastered, then they come up with one more thing: you have to make a great endowment to the religious/philosophical organization or some other organization, and then they will pray for you.

You do not need someone else to pray for you. You *do* need to pray for yourself. You do need to recognize the inner Self, the divine Self, and to speak with that divine Self often.

That is what prayer is. It is to speak with the inner Self. You can call it speaking to God as you pray, but the God-Self is within you. You can say that you are praying to me, but I am One with you and I am within you, so truly you are praying to the within of yourSelf, the inner being of you. And you use prayer for clarification.

You pray with words, with ideas, and then you listen. That is meditation. So many of you and the brothers and sisters pray all the time lots of words; I hear them. And then when the answer may be coming to you, you close it off and you run somewhere because you have to do something, or you do not realize that truly you have the power to know the inner Self, to know the Truth of your Being.

So when you pray—it is a very good thing to pray—you are clarifying for yourself the situation. And you can pray for a certain outcome. There is nothing wrong in praying for a certain outcome, a visioning, if you will. Make the visioning come from the highest and best for all concerned; for yourself and for all others who seem to be in that vision with you.

And then meditate on what you have been praying for. Listen. Be still, and hear the Voice within. Do not be in a big hurry to rush off and do. The doing will take care of itself.

It takes some practice. I am not saying it is easy. It takes some practice, but not a whole lot. Not more than what you can do, because again, it is your reality and it is your power, so you are changing things, and if you say that the vision is going to take a while to manifest…there is a saying in your world that it takes twenty-one days to change a habit, and if you believe that it takes twenty-one days, it will probably take twenty-one days. But if you say, "Well, heck, I don't have twenty-one days. There is this timeline coming up, and maybe I only have ten days, so I really better focus on ten days," then it will take you ten days.

But maybe you only have three days, so you say, "Okay, I need a miracle," and then you create a miracle and you get it all done in three days. *Whatever you decree, it will be as reality to you.* Remember that, because for so often you have been taught that someone else out there will decree what you have to do and what your reality is. You are making your reality moment by moment.

You are the extension of the one creative Source. That is why you are so creative at doing all of the dramas, all of the realities, all of the things you think you have to wrestle with. But now you are coming to a place of accepting your power and saying, "Okay, I've completed. I've done different stages of life and I'm happy with what I've done. Some of the choices at the time, I wasn't sure if they were right choices or not," but they were, because here you are. It brought you to this place of recognizing the goodness of you.

Every stage of life presents you with opportunities. Sometimes they do not look like opportunities, but now you are changing how you see things. If you need a new pair of glasses, go out and get a new pair of glasses to allow you to see things differently. Try it. You can take the sunshades off. And will you be blinded by your own light? Yes, probably, for a moment or so, but then you adjust. It will be okay. Play with whatever tools you can come up with that allow you to recognize the divine Self—capital "S"—that is you.

This is what I spoke unto you two thousand years ago as you were my disciple. I had more than twelve disciples, you know. My goodness, would I limit myself? No. And they were not all men. Now, I had a lot of men friends, as I do in this day and time, but I also had in that day and time and now a lot of women friends. And sometimes the intuitive feminine grasped my message more quickly than the masculine energy that wants to know the logic of how to put A, B, & C together.

So sometimes you have to put to one side the mental and allow yourself to abide in the feminine love that says, "I love myself, even if I am not perfect; and Jeshua tells me I *am* perfect. Well, maybe he's right. I listened to him before, and sometimes he was right. And maybe if he was sometimes right, maybe he can be right in more times than just one or two times." And I assure you that I *am* correct in telling you of your divine nature.

Did I prophesy? No. Possibilities, probabilities, maybe. Do I prophesy in this day and time? No. Do you know why

I do not prophesy? Because I do not have the power to tell you what you are going to choose in the next moment. I have seen you in your creative improv. I can say unto you that next week on the middle day of the week called your Wednesday at one o'clock in the afternoon there is going to be a bolt of lightning—metaphysical, that is—that is going to strike you down to the place where you are going to have a new understanding. Maybe this will happen. Maybe it will not; maybe it will be *two* o'clock in the afternoon. It will be as you decree. So I do not prophesy and I do not give over my power to prophecies.

Now, I would do with you a meditation. Allow the eyes to soften. Allow yourself to take the deep breath that brings you to a place of peace within. Allow yourself to come to the place of peace that the world does not know, the place of peace that your divine Self *does* know; the place of peace where you can step back from everything that is happening, everything that *has* happened, everything that you have anticipated that might happen; the place of peace that is the eternal Now.

That is where you abide, in the place of the eternal Now, forever going forward in the Now. Breathe peace into the Now. Breathe peace into *your* Now, and know the peace that is your divine inheritance as the one holy Child; not separate from your peace. Know the peace of your being.

Know that truly you are loved with an everlasting love that will never forsake you, because you will never forsake *it.*

Always you will abide in love. Always you will abide as One, one holy Now.

And taking another easy breath, bring to mind something that has been in your reality that seems like you would have to think about it, have to dwell upon it perhaps; bring it into the peace, keeping the peace of the Now with you. Allow yourself to abide in peace and to look at whatever the issue seems to be.

Reach out and take that issue by the hand. Walk with that issue as friend to friend. Walk with that issue to the very edge of the hologram that you have called your reality. Walk with that issue hand in hand to the very edge. And looking down from the edge of that reality that you have said has to be so true—lower case "t"—look down and see the space that is below; only space, openness, undefined. Look across and see the space before you, open, undefined. Look above and see the space that is open above you; eternal space filled with love, filled with trust, filled with knowing of divine Is-ness.

For wherever you go, hand in hand with whatever seems to be an issue, you walk into the divine Is-ness of you, undefined as yet, and all is within your power. So you turn to the issue and you say, "Shall we go forward?" You walk into the space of peace of the eternal Now, and the issue that seemed so threatening, so complex, so unknowable becomes as a no-thing. It becomes part of you. You have accepted it into yourself as part of the peace of your Now.

There is nothing to fear; no space below, no space across, no space above that would be fearsome; only peace abides in the space around you. That is the key and the power of your peace.

Always you abide in the eternal Now and the eternal peace of the Now, and any issue you take into that peace will become as your friend, will become as part of you and dissolve into the love of your heart. Any issue; take it into your heart and love it and feel it dissolving in the love and in the peace. Know that no thing, no person, no circumstance, no issue has power over you.

You have created what you thought to be something to walk with you, and you have reached out your hand and you have taken the hand of that issue and you have said, "Come with me to the edge of reality and let us look upon the space of the eternal Now, open, as yet undefined."

Breathe. Know peace. Breathe. Feel peace. Breathe. Know that you are creating everything in your reality; therefore, you can mold it, shape it, change it. You can take it by the hand and lead it into your heart and dissolve it in love, for it has no power over you. You have created it, and you can re-make it in love.

And now taking another deep breath, allow the consciousness to come back to the body. Feel the peace where you have been and bring it back with you. Feel the power of the nothingness of any issue, for it is a friend, and you can take a friend into your peace and dissolve it in love. Bring the consciousness back to this room. Bring the consciousness back to the body.

Know that truly you abide in the peace of the eternal Now, open and undefined until you choose a definition. It is a gift that you weave into your reality. Acknowledge it often, for the peace of the as-yet-undefined eternal Now is the Truth—capital "T"—of your being. And in that space of great peace I join you as the One—one creative extension of All That Is.

So be it.

HOW DO I LOVE THEE?

"How do I love thee? Let me count the ways." Yes, you have a very famous writing which has stood the test of time. I love you because I know That Which you are. I love you because I love myself, and I *am* you. Take that deeply into the consciousness.

I, whom you have seen to be an individual who had a lifetime a long time ago, I *am* you, and I am living your lifetime as you see your reality now to be—lowercase "r". I live *through* you and *as* you, and *with* you as the One that we are.

"Well, how can that be?" you ask. "I mean, he's one Yeshua. He's one Jesus who was a fully realized human being. He knew who he was as spirit, and I don't know that. From time to time I really feel quite human."

Well, I will say unto you that in my lifetime as one Yeshua I knew human reality; I knew human emotions. You have it recorded in your holy Scriptures that I looked upon Jerusalem and knew the conflict which was going on there, and I wept.

I even knew jealousy. Early on in life I compared myself to my cousin John, the one you know as the Baptist. He was bigger, taller, a bit older than I, and I knew jealousy until I realized that we all have different qualities and yet we come from the same Source.

I took a deep breath and I sat by flowing water and watched the water as spirit flowing. I became One with the water to the place where it did not really matter that my cousin John was bigger than I, could run faster than I, climb a tree faster and easier than I. It did not really matter, because I knew myself to be ongoing spirit, Life itself.

I knew the human emotions. I knew frustration when I could see a better vision, and I overturned the money changers' tables. I wanted to make a point: I wanted to make a point to them where they would stop and perhaps think that there could be another way to do things.

I knew how it felt to be tempted by the world. You have the quotation in your holy Scriptures where I said, "Get thee behind me, Satan." In other words, "Do not bring temptation to me to live in separation in the small egoic self. I do not want it. Get thee behind me." Let it be in the past.

I also understood the opportunity to entertain the feeling of fear. Again, you have it recorded in your holy Scriptures that I prayed in the Garden of Gethsemane that, "If it be possible, let this cup pass from me; nevertheless, not as I will, but as Thou wilt."

So, you see, I knew human emotions. But I also knew what you are coming to know: that none of those emotions is lasting. You may get very upset with someone and you may feel that you really, really want to shout to the heavens; and yes, I have heard you when you have been shouting to the heavens. But then the energy passes.

You are like the volcano which erupts with the energy of emotion, but I have also seen you calm the volcano. I have also seen you ask for better vision. "What is truly going on here?" you have asked. "I want to see the whole picture. I want to see much more than what has just pushed my buttons," as you like to call it.

You are moving into a space of expanded consciousness. You have come to a place of wanting to abide in the heart, to abide in stillness and in peace, to abide in love and understanding, to know that brothers and sisters may choose other choices than the ones you would make, but they are doing their completions and they are following their divine path at this time as they see it.

So allow yourself to be at peace always and anywhere you find yourself to be. You are as the ripples on the pond, because as you come to a place of peace within yourself, it ripples out and touches other ones.

Conversely, when you are upset and emoting, that is also felt by the brothers and sisters, and they may have to leave you for a while—or they may join in, because human drama is an adrenaline rush and it is exciting. It proves to you, if you need any proof, that you are living a reality, and it feels very important.

But then, when you have done this enough times, you come to a place of saying, "Okay, I know that road. I know where it leads. I don't have to go that way. I can if I want to," and you can, "but I don't really need to. I've been down that road before many times. So I can take a deep breath."

And with the deep breath comes peace. If it does not come right away, breathe again and again and again until finally you may even fall asleep, and that is okay. You have come to a place of peace which allows you to be asleep for a while to allow the body to relax. And when you awaken, you will not be in the same place where you were emotionally before the time of sleep.

I love That Which you are, because I *know* That Which you are. I know that you are divine Love, divine Light, divine spirit going forward one more time into a reality that you are making for yourself, a reality that yet believes in duality and all of the gradations between the best and the most terrible. And you know how those emotions feel.

I love you as I love myself. Now, I would exhort you to love yourself. You have a teaching which has come down through the ages through your religious/philosophical organizations which has commanded you to love me, to love Jesus and to love God with all your heart, with all your mind, with all your soul, with all your being.

You have done the best that you could do with that, but it has been yet placing your love outside of yourself, loving me or God as separate and above you. Love yourself. Take time in every day to say the words, "I love myself. I really love me. I really love my life."

And if separated ego runs in and says, "Yes, but what about...etc.," you take the deep breath and you say, "I love the divine Self of me. I am having a human experience," and you are, "and it is good. And I love the fact that I have the courage to have a human experience."

I have said to you many times that I honor you because of the courage it has taken to choose one more incarnation in a reality which does not believe totally in love—or even a small bit sometimes.

I love That Which you are because I know Who and What you are: the extension of the one creative Principle. I have shared with you many times how I enjoy—I live in joy—to watch you—me, as I am within you—handle the different situations in life and how soon you rise up over what may be a tripping point and how soon you come back to the place of centeredness which says, "I Am That Which I Am. I Am All. I Am One. I am One with Yeshua. I am One with Mother Mary. I am One with my brother. I am One with my sister."

That is an interesting thought, and it is true. Because, as I have said to you over the many, many years I have spoken with you, *there is no separation.* Now, do you think I say that over and over just to hear myself? No. I say it to you because it is true. There is no separation.

I am you; you are me expressing the creative Principle. I live within you. I am not on the cross. I am not outside of you somewhere to be adored, to be loved as a separate entity. I live through you *as* you. I have said to you many times, "I walk *with* you *as* you."

And you have said, "Oh, that sounds nice, but I don't know what that means. I'm facing all of these choices and challenges and Yeshua would know what to do, but I don't know what to do, so therefore I guess, well, maybe he's over here; maybe he's really close; he might even have his arm around my shoulder. But to be One with him, with That Which he is? I don't know how that would be."

Yes, you are, and I Am, One. "Deep, really deep," you say, and yet it is simplicity itself. Everything that you encounter is the creativity of you. Everything that you bring into your reality, your hologram—as we have spent time talking about the hologram that you make, the illusion of reality, lowercase "r"—I am in that with you, as well. Never do you walk alone.

Now, I know separated ego says, "Oh, yeah, well, he can say that, but you know, I feel really alone." Have you ever looked at your word "alone" and taken it apart? All one; alone. All One.

So at your times of feeling most alone, allow yourself the deep breath and say, "Yeshua, I'm sure glad that you're with me, that you *are* as me, that *we* are going together as One through this lifetime."

The energy that you are is not contained within the body. Bodies are separate as they seem to be defined by the edge of the skin, but your body truly does not even end there. There is what is termed the aura that you already know about, and your energy goes out farther than that, in any case, and blends with everyone else's.

I Am that energy. I Am spiritual energy, as you are. That is how I can be within and as you and everyone else. There is no limitation. Bodies suggest limitation, but in truth, there is no limitation. There is no separation.

So when you awaken in the morning, allow yourself to welcome me to walk with you throughout the day. I will be doing it anyway, but it is nice to be acknowledged. I cannot go anywhere apart from you. Even if I wanted to, which I do not, I could not, because we are all divine energy, spiritual energy.

The matrix out of which we form that which we experience is creative divine energy. It is called love. And as you allow yourself to acknowledge the love that you are, it expands and you begin to understand what the words have been telling you. Words are clues. The words I have spoken unto you for a long, long time have been Truth. There is no separation. I live through you *as* you. Therefore, I love That Which we are.

How do I love thee? With a most expansive, unlimited, immeasurable—because it is unlimited—love. It is the love of the Father, Abba. It is the love of the Mother. It is the love of spirit. It is the love any way that you want to define it. It is that and more, because truly no definition can limit the Love that you are.

I love the ocean of Love that we are, and there is nothing else to do except be That Which we are. Yes, you can struggle with all the ups and downs of the world. You can have projects that you want to work on, and that is good, especially if you bring the Light of your consciousness to it, the love of your consciousness, and that you use as your touchstone for any project that you give your energy to, "Is this done in love? Is this done to further the expansion of love?"

Then stand back and do not judge, because there may be—as we have spoken so often—a bit of improv that comes in. You may think, in separated ego terms, that you have it all worked out. You have been there, where you had it all worked out, and then something happened, a little bit of improv that perhaps somebody threw in there and you said, "Well, I have to go back to square one and start over with this again."

Well, truly, you never go back to square one, but you do the improv and you do make changes and you do expand. So whenever there may be a bit of a quirk that is thrown into a project, allow yourself to say, "Okay, this is for my expansion. I will have a new perspective out of this, even if I did not expect a new perspective."

Then allow yourself to rejoice—to take the deep breath and to be in peace. Joy and peace are your divine nature, and that is what you are connecting with as the awakened Christ.

How do I love you? With an eternal love that cannot even be measured; it cannot be measured in quantity or in time. It can only be acknowledged.

I love That Which you are: a deep abiding Love. I Am you, and you are me. You are within the divinity of One. And yes, you often play the drama of being, "Well, I'm only human," but you are much more than that. You are the Love which has existed from before we created time, and you are the Love which will always be, even after the purpose of time has been fulfilled—forever and always as One.

How do I love thee? With a great abiding understanding, and awakening of the Love that we are; the one divine extension; the One so loved that it could never be abandoned, only acknowledged and honored.

So be it.

THE QUESTIONS BASIC TO YOUR REALITY

Beloved one, now I would speak with you about questions, questions that are basic to your reality, questions that come up.

Oftentimes you will be asking these questions of yourself, and many times ones are asking these questions of me, questions such as, "Who am I? I awaken in the morning and I seem to remember the person I was the day before. I get up and I do what is accustomed on that day, whatever the schedule will say that I am to be doing."

And yet at the same time you feel that persona is not all of you. You feel that it is part of you. It is in truth an act, as you are the actor/actress playing a certain part in what you see to be reality—lowercase "r"—and you do it very well.

You remember the personality from the day before and the day before and the day before, and maybe you will do a bit of reshaping and changing during the day as there may be new friends who come with some new ideas. And you may change what seems to be the personality as you go through different stages of life.

"Who am I?" You are the extension of the one divine Source. You are the extension of the one Mind, the one...I will not even call it Being, because that will identify it with limits, but of one universal Energy, and yet it is not limited to this universe. You are even more than what this universe will suggest.

"Who am I? I *am* divine. I *am* the creative One—capital "O". I *am* the creative One who is creating my reality—lowercase "r"—each moment as I go through the day and through the night. I am creative, because the one Mind *is* creative." That is Its nature. And you, because you are an extension—I will not say Child, because that implies that there may be a separation between Source and Child—you are an extension of the one creative Mind going forth experiencing Itself.

Some of your wise ones have written about the Mind of God and how It is forever re-creating Itself and expanding, expanding upon what has seemed to be the experience of the day before, the year before, the time before. And this is true, because you want to know, "What else is there?" So beyond the fulfillment of the purpose of time there will yet be expansion.

You are, even as you see yourself to be contained within the skin of the body, much more than just what you see. There is what your scientists have shown you: the aura of energy around you. They have taken photographs of the different colors of the aura as you have been in different emotional states, and you have seen how this can shift and change.

That is part of what you are, and yet you are more than that. Your scientists are not yet at the place of being able to register more than just what is quite dynamic around you. Your energy expands farther than you can imagine, and there will come a time when you will know that energy. You will know yourself to be unlimited energy, unlimited… I will call it Love.

Separated ego says, "I don't want to know all of that, because I am fairly familiar with this body and this personality and this life that I am living. Yes, I would make some changes with it, but maybe I don't want to know how expansive my energy is. Maybe I will be lost."

Ones have a fear of releasing the physicality because they feel that maybe they will be lost in the void somewhere and no longer exist. Well, that is not true. That cannot be. You will exist forever and forever and forever and beyond forever, because you *are* the creative Energy.

So you will keep on keeping on, but it will not be a persistence that says, "I have to." It will be a persistence of keeping on because you want to, because you are so excited about, "What else can I create? Where else can I go? Who else can I interact with? And what more technology can I find where I can be creative and I can be in touch with ones who may not be right in front of me, or maybe they are? And I can be creative in ways that I have yet to explore."

"Who am I? Am I just a speck of dust rattling around in a big universe? Am I going to get lost?" No, you can never be lost. Separated ego can say to you that there is a possibility that you might be lost somewhere and that you would never be found, but separated ego is just that. It is separated from its Source, and it tells you only what it knows in separation. The Oneness of you, when you touch that space, knows Itself to be All and to be expansive and to be forever ongoing and creating.

So then the next question comes up: "*Why* am I? What is my purpose?" That question is asked so many times. "What is my purpose? I'm living a life, I'm doing the best I can with it, with all of the challenges. Sometimes friends and coworkers offer me a challenge, but I don't always have to take what they want to give me. They are very free in giving, but I don't always have to take it. What about what the body wants to give me? Do I have to take that? *Why* am I living this life? What is my purpose?"

Your purpose is to be alive, to be happy, to be joyful, to be the Light that you are, to be creative, and to know that you are the one who is creating your reality moment by moment by moment. And if you do not like what you are creating, then stop and write a new script, because you are the one who is writing the script in the first place. If you do not like it, stop.

There is no one and no thing that is more powerful than you are. The world is not more powerful than you are, although the *voice* of the world may scream that it is more powerful and the body may scream that it is more powerful, but you are the creator of the world and the body. You are the one who has agreed that you would express for a temporary time with the physicality, with the body, the molecules of the dust of our holy Mother Earth, and that you will activate a body so that you can walk amongst the brothers and sisters, give them hugs, talk with them, be in relationship with them, be in joy, truly in joy with them, because you *are* the all-powerful One.

Now, I know that the world does not say that to you. The world says everything is a challenge, and you will have to do the best you can with it, and you do. But the world is of your making. You are making your world as you go along. As you wake up in the morning, before you hop out of bed, or before you *fall* out of bed sometimes, visualize how you want your day to be. It only takes a moment or so. You do not have to spend fifteen minutes, one-half hour in bed. You do not have to even get up and sit in a certain position and breathe through one nostril and face the east or the west or whatever. You do not have to have ritual about it.

Just pause for a moment as you wake up and visualize how you want that day to be. If you know the people that you are going to be interacting with that day, visualize meeting them and speak with them heart to heart, mind to mind, before you even put the feet on the floor. And you will find that truly the day will be different because you have decreed that it is going to be different.

So if there is some challenge that you are working with, allow yourself to look at it as a gift, because everything you make for yourself *is* a gift. It has a blessing in it, and the blessing is to rise up over it and to know that you have brought it about. And if you have brought it about—and I assure you that you have—then you can re-create it and change it.

Even if separated ego says, "No, you can't change that; it is too difficult, too complex, too many people involved, too much of the world saying that this is how it has to be," you can change it. You do it by allowing the feeling to arise within you that, "I Am all-powerful. I Am the creative One. I Am the extension of the one Creator, and I create this day in joy. I'm going to enjoy it. I don't care what else happens. I'm going to enjoy it." I know that there are some days when the body says, "Oh, yeah, right." But you can still enjoy it.

So *who* am I? The extension of the one creative Source, the one Mind. *Why* am I? For the purpose of living in joy.

Who are *you*? Why are *you* in my world? You are in my world so that we can interact, get together; we can give the hugs, we can give the shoulder if one needs a shoulder to rest upon, or the ear to listen to someone's story. You are in my life because I have created you to be in my life.

Now, you have your own individuality, as you understand reality—lowercase "r"—so that you are not controlled by my thinking that you are in my world. You *are* in my world, but you also have the power to not be in my world. In just a moment you can step out; you are free to get up and walk out if you want to. Or you can absent the mind; your body is still in my world, but you are not.

So *why* are you? You are for the purpose of bringing joy. Now, there have been lifetimes when you have lived a solitary life and you have said, "I don't want anybody else in my life. I'm going to live in this cave all by myself. I have everything I need. I manifest it for myself." And that has been okay for a lifetime or two or three or twenty. But then you have come to a place where you have said, "I wonder what else there is to experience. I wonder if there is someone else like me. I wonder if there is someone else not like me. I wonder...." And as soon as that small idea comes—"I wonder"—immediately everything changes, and it changes for the good.

Now, separated ego, again, will say, "Look, things may not be perfect, but don't change anything, because I am comfortable with these things that aren't really perfect. So don't go rocking the boat."

But I say unto you, go ahead and rock the boat. What happens if the boat turns over? You walk on water. You are the one creating the water. What is to keep you from walking on it if you want to? You do this already when you have the rainy day and you have some puddles of water out there. You walk on water. No big deal. Just because you think maybe it is a bit deeper, it might be a big deal, but not really. The principle is still the same.

You can walk on water. I did, and you have. But you have come to this lifetime saying, "Okay, now I want to forget most of what I've done in other lifetimes so that I can experience things anew." You start out as the small infant that ones have said is a *tabula rasa*; in other words, a blank slate.

But truly, no small one comes without their own personality traits. You see in the same family that there may be one who is really right there up in your face, and another one who is a little more timid and says, "Will it be alright if I…?" They are in the same biological family, but they have remembrances and moldings from what you would term previous lifetimes.

Who am I? *Why* am I? Who are *you*? *Why* are you? Because it is to play together, to be in joy together, to understand that you are the One expressing as the many. Truly there is only One of us. It is the one extension of divinity. But we have created many so that we can play with each other.

We tried being solitary. It was okay as a solitary God, but after a while we wanted to know more. Always the God Self wants to express Itself and experience Itself in many other ways. So I have created all of you to be with me in this adventure.

Now, that brings me to a very good point. How about loved ones who have passed on? Are they gone? Of course, they are not gone. There is no place to go to outside of the One—capital "O"—that we are. So they are right here always with you, loving you, understanding you in ways that they did not seem to when there was the human interaction going on.

If you find yourself perhaps singing a song that reminds you of a loved one—"That was their favorite song; they really liked that song." Well, they are right there singing it into your ear, reminding you, "I'm here."

The beloved pets that you also create for companionship and for joy see other dimensions. Sometimes you will see the beloved pet looking around and you ask, "Well, what do you see? Who do you see?" They may not tell you, but you can intuit who and what is going on.

Beloved ones never leave you. When you decide that you want to release the body and absent yourself from this interaction, you will always be with me. "Lo, I am with you always, even unto the end of the world." In other words, unto the ending of the belief that there could be separation.

"Lo, I am with you always, even unto the end of the world," and especially after the end of the world. Then there will come the knowingness of Oneness, of joy, of not having to overcome anything.

The world loves to make judgment, and the world loves to say that marriage, commitment, relationship means "until death do us part." Well, that is true—until the death of that relationship. Then you move on. You then come into a new reality—lowercase "r".

Is there a God? Yes. In this reality you believe that there is a God, and you have many definitions of God. That is why you have so many different religious gatherings where the one who is in authority will stand up and tell you what you believe about God. You are seeing now some clashes, unnecessary, but yet they have been brought about so that you can examine who and what is God.

Is there a God, first of all, and the answer is Yes. *Who* is God? Everything you see. *What* is God? It is the divine one Mind going forth to express and experience Itself, and how It does this is in a multitudinous variety of ways; many different varieties. And it is all God.

We have talked quite a bit recently about the hologram that you make for yourself; in other words, the reality—lowercase "r"—that you make for yourself. And it is as a hologram that is playing out in front of you as you allow yourself to step back from it far enough to behold it in that way. It is a reality in which you function, and it is at the same time an illusion.

A book which I have dictated, *A Course in Miracles,* speaks of the illusion. I speak now of another word for it, of the hologram that you are making for yourself and how you can behold that hologram right in front of you in a moment or so of Oneness, where you step back from it and you say, "Hey, I can see what is going on...."

And with that feeling, that knowing, you are often right back into it again. But as time—again, a construct that you have made in this reality—goes on, you come to a place where you stay in the place of Beholder longer and longer, where you know that everything truly serves the remembrance of the at-One-ment, the atonement; not atonement because you have done everything wrong and you somehow have to atone for it and you have to be down on the knees and say so many rituals, etc., not that kind of atonement.

The atonement which I speak of is the remembrance of at-One-ment where you know yourself to be the One, and only; the extension of the one and only creative Principle. Now, the mental mind loves to play with words, with concepts and constructs that you make. The mental mind tells you that you are limited. You are limited by the body and what it feels like. You are limited by the personality that you have defined. You are limited by time; that is one of the big limitations that you have built-in to this reality. And why have you built it in? So that you can then leave it, so that you can say all time is Now.

"I Am the breath of Spirit. I don't have to worry about getting home at a certain time and allowing the body to rest for X number of hours so that I am refreshed and ready to go on the next day and to tackle everything that the world is going to throw at me. Hey, maybe I'm free." With the breath of Spirit, you *are* free.

You have heard stories of wise ones who do not sleep at night. They may spend an hour in meditation and then they are refreshed. They may not even call it meditation, but they allow themselves to come to a place of peace where they know Oneness with Self—capital "S"—and they know that they are in tune with everything that happens, everything that they create. Those are the ones who often *are* your creators who bring forth the inventions, because in that state of peace and receptivity, new ideas for creating something more come in.

Many think they are limited by the geographical miles from a place. But in time, and beyond time, you will come to the realization that you are the one creating any and all limitations. That is the point I would like you to take from this message: that you are creating your reality, and **your questions help you realize your Reality.**

Imagine if you had one million marbles of all different colors and they were in a huge glass bowl. That is just a symbol of what your realities are. You reach in and you take a marble. Maybe it is a purple one, and you say, "Wow! That is really, really pretty, but I like the red one, too," and you take the red one. And then, "Oh, I like the clear one," so then you take a clear one.

You have all of the million marbles in the glass bowl to choose from, and you are allowed to pick *any* of them and all of them. There is no limit. That is what you are doing day by day, as you understand time and days, as you understand your reality.

Everything is right there for you. Just visualize it; know that it is in that huge glass bowl and it is going to come to you. And then when it comes to you, jump up and down like a little child and say, "Wow! It happened. It really happened!" And the joy in you is made complete.

That is truly *Who* you are. That is *Why* you are.

So be it.

THE BASIC LAW OF THE UNIVERSE

Beloved one, you are coming into a time now which is part of a progression that has started a long time ago—even before this lifetime as you measure lifetimes—a progression of allowing expansion, of allowing the Awakening and a feeling of lightness, more Light.

That is why you are seeing elemental darkness in your political arena and in many of the areas that you look at. The darkness is coming up now in the dramas, and you think, "Oh, it's getting worse," but it is not.

All of the things that have been swept under the carpet and held under the carpet because it was thought not safe to talk about them, think about them, or to bring them out into the light are now coming out into the Light in order to be healed. It is as you would have perhaps the skinned knee. It looks terrible. It is all skinned up, bruised, and you think, "What's happening? It's all a mess."

Well, that is what you are living with in the world. It is coming to a place where it has been scraped down to perhaps the bloody bit of it and it looks pretty awful, but what it has to do now is to heal. It is coming to a place where, if you have had an infection and a swelling under the skin, it has to open, and then the healing can happen. That is what you are seeing, the whole messy bit under the skin now being exposed, and that is when the healing can start.

So when you hear of the infection of the world, allow yourself to know that truly the skin is being pulled back so that the healing can begin to take place.

It is happening not only in your geo-political grouping, but also in all of the others, and because now that you are coming to a threshold of understanding Oneness, you are aware of all of the brothers and sisters in other geo-political groupings who are rising up and making quite a bit of turmoil so that it looks terrible, and yet what is happening is working towards the healing.

Now, we have acknowledged that your timing seems to be quite slow. Verily, many changes happen every day, and they all add together to bring the collective consciousness to awakening. Sometimes it takes a while before ones can see, "Oh, we are now further along than we were maybe six months ago or two years ago. You know, there's been some evolution which has happened."

It takes a while before it is obvious. So ones can say, "Well, this is really terrible. Every day when I turn on my television set, I get to see news that is just really, really disheartening," and yet the heart is in it. The heart is the healing of bringing it out into the light so that the healing can begin.

So when you feel disheartened, know that truly you are putting the heart back into it. When ones will give you the news which sounds like fresh disasters—and there is always a new one every day, or several every day perhaps—know that truly it is being brought to your attention. You are inviting it to come to your attention so that you can know the truth of it; not to focus on the obvious; do not deny that there is violence happening, or perhaps there are ones who have all of the possessions swept away in the wind—and yet you have seen these ones when they have been asked, "How is it for you?" they say, "I am blessed because I have come through this."

And so ones awaken. Ones then come to a place of understanding, "It is my divinity that truly orchestrates my life." And when that "Aha!" happens, then there is great laughter. There is a throwing off of the heaviness of the world and in comes a feeling of Light. At that moment the aura expands quite significantly and they can go with a step that is lighter, that is free.

I speak to you from a place of freedom, of expansiveness. I want you to grasp the feeling of expansiveness, because it is your true divine nature. The basic law of the universe is expansion, always and forever expanding.

Your scientists, when they look at the known universe, have told you that it is expanding outward. Your inner nature is expanding as well. The basic nature of *you* is to expand.

You are energy. Truly everything is energy. Whether it is formed or unformed, it is energy, and the basic law of energy is to expand. That is why you are making for yourself new universes, the ones within and the ones that are seen and measured by your scientists.

In your life you can feel the underlying current of life energy and know that it is always going forward, expanding as the energy of spirit. First of all, it goes into the mind and you play with the creative current in the mind. Then, with the deep breath you can come to the *feeling* of the current of living energy. That is why I say unto you to take the deep breath, because when you take that deep breath, you allow yourself for a millisecond to touch the current that is underlying everything.

So whenever you remember to take the deep breath you allow yourself to go to the place that truly is the underlying divinity, the current that is always you and will forever be as you go forward into what you see to be other experiences, other lifetimes, other forms, other manifestations of whatever you want to bring forth.

Allow yourself to know that, "I Am eternal"—because you are. "I Am the spirit that activates everything that I see. I Am divine. I Am of the Creator. That is why I am so creative. Oh, my goodness, sometimes I wish I weren't so creative." But then you take the deep breath and you say, "Well, that which I have judged to be not so good—I could have done better"...then you see how even the place where you say, "I could have done better," has brought you to the place where you understand that you now *are* better.

Everything builds with a purpose. Everything builds to bring you to the place of accepting in awareness, true awareness, "I am okay. Everything I have thought that maybe I could have done better was actually perfect at that time." Even I, as Jeshua two thousand years ago, sometimes thought, "Oh, I could have done better; I should have said...."

I knew the power and the peace and the love of the Father, and I wanted to give it to people. I wanted them to come alive in it. Some of them caught it, but many of them did not. They were caught up in thinking, "What do I have to do tomorrow? Where am I going to get the golden coins?"

So I prayed to the Father—I did more than pray to the Father; I spoke quite loudly to the Father—and I said, "What's wrong? What's wrong with me that I can't get the message across? I love these ones. I love this one. I want him to know how beloved he is. I want him to feel it, truly feel it deep within himself."

And when I stopped and I took finally a deep breath, the Father said to me, "There is nothing wrong with you, and there is nothing wrong with the ones who do not understand right now. They are in their right place on their journey. You are saying the right thing, and in time they will hear those words. Maybe two thousand years have to go by, maybe even longer, but it is okay. There is nothing wrong with you."

So I took the deep breath and I said, "Well, if you say so, I guess You know," speaking with and to my divine Self, which is the Father. So I went forward speaking my truth of the love of the Father, the goodness of the Father, how life can be lived easily and happily, even though the Romans were coming with their swords and demanding that ones give up not only the golden coins, but their dwelling places, even their physical bodies. They were exerting what they [the Romans] saw to be their power at that time.

But it was only passing temporal power, and now you have the advantage. You can look back and say, "That's part of history. I see how they rose up and they were in power for a while, but that was passing." And there have been other civilizations that have arisen and passed away. You have some that are known now in what is called your mythology, ancient history, even before recorded history, and it is all true.

Over and over you reinvent until you come to the place of the deep breath. You come to the place of saying, "Look at what I have come through. Look at the lifetimes that I have lived. Look at what I have done, all of the other lifetimes where I have been a leader, where I have given of my vision and sometimes of my body, because that was what was needed. I've really come a long way. It *is* expansion that is forever going forward."

And you have heard me speak over and over about going forward and expanding and experimenting and expressing until the purpose of time has been fulfilled, because you are going to go outside of time. Time is a construct that you have built into this reality, and you feel it to be constricting from time to time—a pun there—you feel it to be constricting and you say, "I can't get everything done in time. I can't get to wherever I want to go in time."

Everything is measured in time in this reality, but you are going to come to a place where you are going to walk out of time. However, you will still be ever expanding, ever expressing, ever creating, because that is your divine nature. So *if* that is your future—and I assure you that it is—you might as well be happy about it. It is a good future, and you *will* be happy in it every day, every moment, even outside of time.

For truly, when you lay down the body you have an experience called heaven, but it is just that, an experience. And when you have experienced it to the place where you feel complete, the same as when you feel complete with the physical expression, you will move from what is called heaven into another experience, ever expanding.

You *are* a galaxy in yourself. Within yourself you are the galaxy. You can see this as you attract certain ones to yourself and you all spin in the same direction, or sometimes you do not and then it feels different. You are a galaxy unto yourself, forever expanding and going forward just for the experience of it, just to know how creative you can be, just to enjoy.

Verily, you are creative energy. Sometimes you wake up in the morning and you say, "Oh, I don't have any energy." Or sometimes you wake up in the morning and you say, "Wow, I can't wait to get up and go do…" whatever you have planned for that day. And you know even in that small example that you are energy; not that you *have* energy, but that you *are* energy. You are creative expansive energy forever going forward, and it will always, even beyond time, be Who and What you are.

To use the word "who" limits it, seemingly as a personality. But to speak of "what" you are, eternal, on-going, beyond even the concept of time, expansive energy—you have called it spirit—that is What you are.

How would it feel to be a man; to have certain attributes of a man; to be masculine; to perhaps be able to ride the great stallion and to know your Oneness with that form of life? How would it feel to be the woman; to be feminine, to birth the small ones? How would it feel to have the physical attributes of the man, yet have the feminine qualities? How would it feel to have the physical form of the woman and have the masculine qualities?

How would it feel to be the butterfly, the very tiny little butterfly, fragile seemingly and yet life itself? How would it feel to be the great wooly mammoth? They are not just part of mythology. Your scientists are now finding some of the remains so that you know that you have brought them forth in what seems to be a long time ago, and you have not only brought them forth; you have *been* them, because you wanted to know, "How does it feel to be so large, expressing so much energy in form?"

Life is an expression of the creative Energy that you are, whether in form or unformed. Life expression is always expanding, wanting to experience Itself even more, forever ongoing, forever creating, forever expanding. The basic nature of the universe, formed and unformed, is expansion. You are the universe Itself.

So be it.

THE EXPANDING UNIVERSE

Beloved one, in the beginning before time was, you called forth the universe. You called forth this particular solar system with your sun and the known planets, as well as other solar systems and galaxies. You called forth a specific planet that is no longer in this solar system, a planet upon which you did great energy experimentation, and the planet exploded into what you now call the asteroids and formed the asteroid belt. You have made changes, and you are in the midst of making more changes; perhaps not quite so physically dramatic as that.

As we have spoken in one of the previous messages, your universe is expanding. Your scientists have verified this as they have measured energy. Truly everything *is* energy. You are energy in form, and you use it in a certain density so that you can walk amongst the brothers and sisters.

Furthermore, you *are* the expanding universe itself. You have put it into physicality so that your scientists, who like to measure, can measure something. And they tell you that the universe *is* expanding, that the relative distance between objects of density is expanding. And that which is in between the more dense objects is the energy of divinity expanding upon Itself. Your scientists are giving you "proof" of what is happening in the outer.

You want to have proof; you always ask to see it in the outer first. "If I can see it, if someone in authority will tell me that it is so, then I will believe it." But truly, as we have spoken many times with you, you are the one creating everything that you experience. So you set in motion a ripple effect of asking what you would like to see, *hoping* that something will happen. And by desiring something, then it starts to manifest, because you have had the idea.

You have had a wish, perhaps not always *knowing w*hat you would like to have, but yet you keep proving to yourself over and over the coincidences of things that happen. And why do certain coincidences of things happen? Because you create; you create everything which you experience.

So as you put out the idea that you want to meet with other ones of like mind, that you want to allow the healing of the body so that it can serve you longer, as you put out that idea, even if you do not really believe it in the first place, the belief grows. And if you will be forthright about what you want to see and what you want to experience, it has to come to you; it has to manifest. For truly, there is nothing, no-thing, no-one who is standing in the way of what you want to create; only yourself as you have said, "Well, this is what I want to create, but I'm going to hold it a little bit away from myself for a while, and then I'll allow it to come closer and closer."

And that is okay too, because sometimes you have an idea of what you want, but it is not complete with all the details in it. As time goes on, you allow some of the shaping and refining to happen. So if it does not come right away, know that truly what you are doing is molding and shaping and making it more to your liking when it does manifest.

Do not give up on the first try. I know that some will get discouraged. They will say, "Well, I tried this affirmation. I was told that it could be true. I said it fifty times, and it hasn't happened yet." Well, there is such a thing as your own divine timing that allows you to refine and to add unto the idea which you had in the very beginning. It allows you time to redefine and to shape and mold it in the way that truly will serve you and others.

There is no accident to anything that you have a desire for. It has come to you for a reason. Abide with it. See it developing and forming, even if it seems to be quite impossible and many of the family and the coworkers and the friends may say to you, "Well, I don't know why you keep holding out for such and such. You know that's not going to be for you."

And yet you do know that it is going to be for you; otherwise, the idea would not have come to you. So abide with it, believe in it, allow yourself to get excited about it. Live with that dream as if you already have it, because you do. Truly, whenever you have an idea and a dream of something that you want to make manifest, abide with it and know that it has come to you for a divine purpose. It will serve you and it will serve many others.

So if you are looking for something—and I know that you have desires and wants and you sometimes think, "Well, it'll happen, but it'll have to be in some future time, some years down the road, perhaps, or it will be when I win the lottery or it will be when there is a sudden shower of the golden coins"—you need not wait. Get started with the planning. Get started with whatever needs to be at the beginning, and you will be surprised at how the other parts come together.

Truly you *are* the one who is manifesting that which you experience, moment by moment by moment. So if you want something, abide with it, play with it, know it to be true, and it happens.

Now, the physical universe is expanding, and the universe within you is expanding. *You* are expanding because you are open to new ideas. You are open to possibilities, even open to probabilities. You start out with a possibility that perhaps this can be, and you think, "Well, you know, there's a probability that this will happen."

It is a great leap of faith when you come to the place of moving from possibility to probability. You have experienced the miraculous feeling of acknowledging that you have moved from possibility to probability. "It's probably going to happen. I'm not quite sure when or how, but it's probably going to happen." And then you get to the place where it is the reality, and it does manifest right in front of your eyes.

Your universe, your inner universe is expanding, and the space between ideas and dreams and wants that you have had over the years is expanding as well. And it is being filled. It is not a void. In your physical universe, the space in between the more dense parts is filled. It is not a void. Your scientists do not quite understand what fills it, but they know it to be energy.

The same is true within your own inner universe. There is no void. There is space which is expanding, and in that space is peace. Abide often with the expansion within yourself and feel the space in between ideas, in between thoughts. Feel the peace and the trust that is in the expanding universe within yourself.

You are moving to a place that acknowledges, "I am energy. I am divine energy. I am creating, I am allowing, and I am peace." The mind will get very busy; the mind loves to be busy. The mind has a role to play, a very good role to play, and it loves to play that role all of the time.

But there are times when you ask it to take a break. "Be quiet for a while, mind. I'll come back to you. Let me just abide in peace. Let me abide in the place that is receptive to perhaps a new idea, a nuance of something that I haven't yet experienced or felt. Allow me to abide in peace and take in new ideas, new hints, as it would be of new ideas. Allow me to feel guidance from the divine Self of me."

For truly, you are never alone. Now, I know separated ego and the mind love to play with being alone and love to say, "You're going to have to really work on this. This is really going to be tough. You've got to use me—the mind—overtime."

And you can do that. You know the feeling of using the mind to the place where you get really, really, really tired—thank goodness—and you stop. You take a deep breath, and on that deep breath comes peace, openness, open to new intuition. It is a gift that you give to yourself: a choice to abide in peace for a while.

You know the clamor of the world: "You need to do this. You're late for that. You have this project that has to get finished. How are you going to do it? You have to make this phone call. You have to abide by this schedule," etc. Finally, you stop and you breathe.

The breath is the first thing you do when you are born into an incarnation. It is the very last thing you do when you leave the incarnation. You have that last breath. And in between, hopefully, you take many more breaths, deep ones that allow peace to be known.

When you are open to the expansion which is happening within, ideas will come to you—ideas of harmony, ideas of nurturing, ideas that are not of the mind, the world mind, but of the divine Mind, ideas that allow you to celebrate Who you are and what you have created.

If you are able—and you are—to step back from yourself and to see yourself as others see you—perhaps a good friend—you will begin to celebrate what you have brought together. Oftentimes separated ego will have much of judgment. It will say, "Well, you didn't finish that project. You haven't brought the body together in the best form that it could be. You should eat more organic. (Smile) You should exercise every day. You should...." It gets to be a bit heavy after a while with all of those "shoulds" piled upon your shoulders.

And then you say, "I'm going to step out of that mold for a moment and look at myself and see myself as my best friend sees me. I am going to *be* my best friend to me, and I'm going to encourage me to do that which I have always wanted to do." For there is nothing holding you back except your choice to perhaps wait a little longer. But you do not have to wait longer. That which you want to manifest is truly right in front of you.

That which you want to manifest, you can, immediately. Or you can wait a few more months until you feel that it has matured a bit. You can either leap right into it, or you can wait a bit and see what else you want to develop, to hone, to refine.

Your physical universe is expanding, forever renewing and expanding, pushing out new frontiers. Your inner universe parallels the physical, forever expanding and renewing, pushing out into new frontiers, new ideas, new perceptions. As your scientists will measure the energy of the physical universe, you will acknowledge an expansion within yourself. Already you have wondered about the new ideas and the resultant manifestations that have mysteriously occurred in your reality. The expansion is going to continue until you will know yourself to be the One creating and experiencing all, both outer and inner. Know that the outer mirrors the inner, and vice versa.

Take these seeming miracles to heart and contemplate where you have been and where you are going. Look far back into the past of this lifetime and see what your beliefs about yourself and others and about the physical were and how the beliefs have changed, morphed and expanded. Look into the future and dream how you would like it to be; how expansive your beliefs about yourself and others and what the world can and will be. Let your consciousness expand into the dream of Love. Know that, as you have a saying in your world—and I paraphrase—whatever you can dream, you can achieve. Dream big.

So be it.

YOUR ROBOTIC SELF

Beloved one, I want to speak with you now about the Love that you are and the robot self of you that you have been. When you are born into physicality, you come as a small infant with remembrances of other lifetimes, other conditionings, other trainings, other events which seemingly have happened.

Then you pick up from the parents what they think is important and true. You live for a while in an in-between state of remembering Home and yet seeing that that does not quite fit the picture of the world, even if it is a small world as you are just a small one, before you have gone to the elementary school.

As time goes on, you become more and more entrenched in generational thinking because that is what you are surrounded by. And then you are thrown into the schooling and you get a wider view of, again, generational teaching and generational thinking, and you unconsciously take on some of those traits. It is not a conscious thing where you say, "Well, I want to know how to hate somebody," but there may be a bully in the class who gives you a hard time and you have feelings of power that come up as anger, then morph into hatred of the other one, because you do not like his/her kind of energy and you want to get away from it, and you become a bit of the robot reacting to situations and actions.

Yet everything that comes to your awareness comes by your invitation, and you are strong enough and powerful enough to deal with it. It comes in perfect timing to help you remember Who you are, to remember the Love that you are and have always been and will always be.

The experiences help you break through the robot self that has only been reactive, coming from a point of the generational teaching. Later you may find yourself being interested in certain teachers, certain friends who are asking the same questions that you are asking, and you find yourself in a new grouping and you begin to leave behind the robot self of you, and you start thinking on your own, "What if? What if that which has been taught to me by my parents and by my peers, what if that isn't all there is to the story or to the picture of life? What if…?"

As soon as that question arises, doors and windows will open for you to see new vistas, to see new ideas, new ways of being. And then, because of the conditioning of the robot self, sometimes the doors and windows will temporarily close again and you find yourself reacting in the old way, but that is okay.

Human experience is not the easiest experience. I know; I tried it, and I ended up on a cross. You also have come through your crucifixions, sometimes physical, many times emotional where you felt you had been nailed to the cross and you were suffering and you wondered if there was any way out of the situation.

Then you did ascend out of it because, out of desperation, you said, "There must be another way. I don't like what is happening right now. There must be another way."

In that moment you gave permission for a new idea to come to you, a new way of feeling about yourself and about others. It turns everything around. It changes everything, whether or not you can see it ahead of time—and usually you cannot—but looking back on it you can see that, "Yes, that was a turning point for me. That was a crucifixion. When my loved one said that he/she didn't want to be with me any longer, when the son/daughter said, 'What you believe is not what I believe,' and walked out of my life, those were hard times of crucifixion."

But they brought you to a place of strength within yourself which you could not deny. You said, "This is who I am. This is what I believe. And no matter what another person believes, no matter how close they are to me, no matter what they say or do, it does not change Who I am and what I believe and what I am striving to remember of Home and of the unconditional Love."

So you have come through those experiences and you have added unto them new experiences which then have added more "evidence" of your divine Self. One small pebble added to another small pebble added to another small pebble…after a while you get quite a pile of pebbles you can build with, step by step, pebble by pebble, little change by little change until finally you look back at the changes and you say, "Wow, what I have done in this lifetime, it's amazing. I would never have thought that I could make such changes, that I could now believe in the Love that I am and that I have to give, and I would never have believed that I would know forgiveness truly deep within myself, forgiveness for all of the other lifetimes when I have been so blinded by the robot self; forgiveness for the words I have spoken that truly another one has invited me to say so that they could come to their own awakening; forgiveness for every choice that I later judged, and forgiveness of self for having forgotten, even temporarily, that which I truly am."

Each one, as you see an individual, is living, walking Love. Each and every individual that you see is here to example divine Love and to remember Home. That is truly what they are seeking, as you are seeking: to know the place where you are okay, where you are accepted, where no matter what you do, say or think, you will always be loved.

You *are* that Love. You have it within you, and oftentimes, because the robot self says to you that it is easier to look outside of yourself, you have been able to give love and to give forgiveness to other ones easier than you could give love or forgiveness to yourself.

Now you are coming to a place of understanding that there is no separation between yourself and the one who sits next to you, the one who sits across the room, the one who lives seemingly miles away from you. Verily, there is no separation.

We have spoken other times of the aura, the light energy that is around you which your scientists can now measure; your photographers can make photographic images of the aura around you. You have begun to understand that your aura expands and intermingles with the auras of ones around you, and even with ones seemingly far away whom you have never met.

As you go through the next few months of your timing, you are going to be seeing more and more of the robot self of others coming up in actions, and you are going to be having opportunity to love them through it. You have seen already much of unrest in some of your geo-political groupings. Even in *this* geo-political grouping there is much of divisiveness and much of ones who will be into judgment.

So in the next several months of your timing you are going to see more of the divisive behavior and more and more words that come from the robot self, the self which is reacting with old thinking, the self which does not understand or want to understand the holier picture.

But the Christ Self will not be denied. There are ones who truly want to change the pattern, who see that what is happening is not for the best evolution of the collective consciousness, and there are enough of you who are seeing past the robot decisions so that you are influencing, just by your visioning, the course of the future.

Right now many are in a robot situation where...well, it has been called "the knee-jerk pattern": something happens and immediately there is a reaction in the old way. But it is coming to a place where there is going to be courage to act differently, to make new choice.

It is difficult when you are surrounded by robotic thinking which has been engrained in you, and then you come into a situation where you are surrounded by it and you are only accepted if you agree to those old-thinking rules. So it take great courage to speak your truth, but you have ones who want to make change, and you are going to see changes happening.

So put on your hard hats, put on your fireproof jackets, and listen to the voice of the world, and yet know that that voice is old thinking. Put forth your own energy into Love and new visioning as to what truly can serve the brothers and sisters.

You have division in this geo-political country, a division which is mirrored in many other geo-political countries, of the ones who have the golden coins wanting to hold onto them. And the ones who do not have the golden coins are saying, "This is not really how it can be." I will not use the word "should", but this is not how it *can* be. There *can* be a more beneficial sharing.

When the collective consciousness changes, you are going to see changes in the ones who have the golden coins. And you are going to call it a miracle when they want to be benefactors and to change the way they do their business.

It is a miracle, and it will occur naturally. It is coming, and you can add your energy to it by knowing that it is coming. Old thinking is passing away because you have decreed that old thinking does not work for everyone.

You have known civilizations and you have been part of civilizations which knew equality and respect one for another. You knew your divinity and you knew that you were playing on holy Mother Earth or on some of the other planets or in some of the other galaxies. You recognized in those civilizations that everyone was from the divine Source.

Separated ego has been your servant in *this* reality many, many times; so much so, that it feels real. And it *is* real—with a lowercase "r"—but it is not Real—with a capital "R". It is part of a construct that you have made as a servant, as a companion to walk with you and to whisper in your ear. Separated ego is very, very good at asking all of the "old" questions. That is what you have programmed it to do. That is part of the robot self. When I spoke of civilizations where you have known equality, where you have known divine expression as everyone comes forth from the one Source, there was a knowing deep inside of you that said, "Oh, I long for that. I know that that is true, and I long for that."

Your longing is going to bring it forth. It is a very strong force within you, the longing to know Home once again and to be free of the robot self that only reacts according to old generational teaching.

Maybe it is not here yet, but your longing is going to bring it forth, because now you are remembering. And once that door starts to open even a little crack of longing and remembering, there is nothing that can stop the Light from coming through that crack in the door, and before you know it, the door opens even further.

So I speak to you of hope. I speak to you of love. I speak to you of remembering your divine Is-ness. I speak to you of Home, and I speak to you of the longing to know the civilizations where you have played without a care because you knew you were playing as the Light that you are. You danced upon the firmament of holy Mother Earth and other planets in other galaxies, and you danced because you were so happy. You deserve to remember that. You deserve to live that once again.

Allow the power that you feel rising up within you, the longing, the remembrance of civilizations when you knew yourself to be divine, when you knew only to dance as the Light. Remember and bring forth that power and express it as love to one another, and you will bring forth miracles. The robotic self will be no more.

So be it.

GOING BEYOND YOUR ROBOTIC SELF: TUNING IN TO GALACTIC ENERGY

Beloved one, I would speak with you about a very interesting and powerful change in energy that is happening now and *will continue for some time.* Your scientists have been studying the stars in your galaxy, the ones in the heavens which you see going into the deepness of the night and into the morning, the ones we watched two thousand years ago together.

Your scientists have been tracking and watching to see the various patterns of the solar system, and you have come to a place now where there is from holy Mother Earth a clear pathway to the center of your galaxy. There is no other solar system between you and the center of what you call the Milky Way galaxy, the galaxy that you are in.

With this alignment, there is now an opening for much energy to be streaming to holy Mother Earth, to your own sun and to your solar system. As you are part, with holy Mother Earth, of the solar system, you are in a direct pathway to access and to feel energy from the very center of your own galaxy. That is what the shift that you have been hearing about for some years now is all about. It is a shift in energy that can be measured and accessed; your scientists are doing that now.

It is an energy that you can use to make great changes within yourself and within everything that is going on in the natural system, nature. All energy, which is what you truly are, is open to you, and the access to it, as there is belief now, is totally open. That is why for some years there has been prophecy of a time when there would be a shift in energy.

You will be seeing many changes in the next twelve months of your timing and beyond, because you are calling forth the changes. Some of the changes you are seeing already, and the progression of changes has to do with awakening. **It has to do with feeling and knowing and using your divine power.**

Now, this has been talked about for thousands of years. I spoke with you two thousand years ago and explained the Love of the heavenly Father—Abba, I called It, as a loving Father—in the terminology of that day and time. For in the culture of that time, the father was the dominant provider and would be the one seen to be providing and protecting. But in this day and time it is more correct to call the energy Father/Mother/God/Goddess/All That Is, so we will go with All That Is.

That energy now is going to be taking various forms, because you are going to be decreeing what you want to see happening in your own individual life. You have ideas, ideas that have come perhaps when you have been working on something else, and you have said, "Well, that would be nice, but I can't because X, Y, & Z."

Yes, now you can, because truly all energy is open to you. The pathway is open, and what you decree is going to be manifesting much more quickly than what you have seen in previous years and in previous lifetimes. So, therefore, it behooves you to perhaps **take out a piece of the notebook paper and write down what you would like to see, how you would like to see it, how it is going to feel, because truly out of the feeling nature comes manifestation.**

Out of the thinking nature sometimes come confusion and complexity, but out of the feeling nature comes manifestation. And then the thinking aspect is brought into play to see, "How do I manifest what I am truly desiring, what I truly feel at home with, what I truly feel excited about?"

Now, sometimes you have already begun to play with options, and the options will continue to expand because you have decreed that you are willing to give up old thinking and to allow the thinking mind to be used by the feeling nature to manifest that which truly is in harmony, that which truly is in love, that which truly is the highest and best that you can visualize for yourself and for others.

Old thinking comes from generational teaching: that which you have been brought up to believe and what the parents were brought up to believe, the old generational teaching of, "This is how it has to be." You are now being freed from that generational teaching, free to choose how you want your life to be.

I will come and whisper in your ear from time to time, "What would *you* like to do? What would you like to see? When would you like to see it? What stands in the way, supposedly, of that feeling of excitement? How can you change that?" I will come and whisper in your ear.

As your belief changes, and it *will* be changing because of the access to direct energy, you will be seeing changes in the physical. A century ago you believed you needed the horse and buggy to take you somewhere. Before that you believed you had to walk, or, if you were lucky, you had a camel or a horse, etc. Now you have manifested the belief in the horsepower *within* the vehicle instead of outside of the vehicle, but it is a belief. Do you see? You have honed it and changed it from what was a century ago, and a century from now you will see even more changes.

But it is not necessary to wait a century. **This year you are going to make great changes because you desire to know your true power and, with that, your freedom.**

So you see how powerful belief is. If you are—and I will use this as an example—in your vehicle and someone else, hopefully, is driving and you are speaking on the device with someone who may be miles and miles away and you are right there with them, because they are describing what they did the night before and how much fun it was, or vice versa, you are not truly with your mind in that vehicle. You are somewhere else.

Then you come back and you say, "Oh, did we go through such and such town?" And the one who is driving says, "Yes, a long time ago." I know you know what I am speaking of: where truly you are not present with what others seemingly are experiencing, because you are somewhere else in your mind.

In the next year you are going to find yourself leaping ahead and wondering, "How did that happen? Something I have wanted to manifest for a long time, I can see how to do it now. If it is something that I want to do on my own, I will see how I can do that. If it is something that I think I want to do with others and manifest it as a 'group project', I will see it coming together easily."

What you want to manifest does not need to be difficult. Only belief holds you in thinking that it has to be a certain way and take a certain time and follow certain steps to get there. But that is just in your thinking. It exists nowhere outside of your mind and the belief system.

What you are going to be doing in the next twelve months of your timing and beyond is going to be exciting, because you are going to be leaving the old belief system behind. You are going to be rushing ahead, jumping ahead to that which you truly have desired, not having to go through a lot of the worldly hoops and hurdles. They may be there for some people, but for you they do not have to be; only as you believe.

Even if you still believe that the world has power over you, you are going to see that power dwindling. You are going to see it becoming as fog. You know what fog looks like. You also know that when you walk out in the middle of fog, it is a no-thing. You can walk right through it, and yet when you stand and look at it, it can seem to be a barrier.

But then you take a step, and you can take another step, and then you take another step and another step, and the fog allows you perhaps not to see exactly what you want to see or as far, but it does not hold you back. And some of the time in this next twelve months, your next year, is going to be a bit like that fog. It is going to perhaps say to you that, "Well, we've always done it this way and it's always had to go through channels and procedures and we've always had to get everybody's approval." But you are going to feel that, "I am a sovereign master. I can walk through the fog. Yes, there are certain things that the world is going to ask of me, but it's not going to be difficult. It's going to be easy."

Your scientists will tell you that it has been thousands of years since the last time when there was a direct pathway with no blockage to the central sun. That is what the Shift has been portending.

Now, the shift that is most important is the shift which happens within you. You will be using some of the physical energy that is streaming to this planet, to this solar system, because there is belief that you can access it. It has been and is being measured, so those of you of logical mind, you can check in on it.

But those of you of feeling nature, you have felt it for some time now, where you have felt, "Things are changing. They're not what they used to be. Some of the things that I thought *were*, aren't, and some of the things that I thought wouldn't be, have come to be."

As you believe, so it will be unto you.

Even if you have only the belief as small as a grain of mustard seed, it will expand and it will grow. If you have the willingness and the belief even as small as the little grain of mustard seed, it will grow as you believe. You realize that out of that seed or out of any seed will come a great plant, a great tree—as you believe.

You are a seedling right now, a most beautiful seedling. You have been growing towards the sun, the central sun as it is known in physicality, and the sun of your own being. You have been growing as the seedling for some time now, because there has been a divine urge within you to know more, to feel more, to feel free, to be able to manifest.

The central sun will help as it is "proof" of energy. We have spoken of the energy that you are many, many times.

You *are* energy. So on a physical level, your scientists will measure and will give you feedback as to the energy that you are. But the sun that you are growing towards is the sun of your own awakening, the sunshine that happens in the morning of your awakening when the seedling comes out of the soil which has nurtured it.

So in what you see to be this next year of your timing, you are going to see many changes come about easily for you. In this next year of your timing, you are going to look back upon *this* time when it was suggested that changes will come easily and you are going to say, "Wow! It really happened. I thought at the time that it sounded really good and I got excited about it and I thought, 'Oh, wow, now that we have this extra energy coming in from the central sun and there's no blockage that way, does that mean it's going to help me clear all of my blockages?'" The answer is, "Yes."

"Does that mean that I'm going to be free to manifest that which I want to?" Yes. "Does it mean that I'm going to change my belief system from the old generational thinking?" Yes. It will be as you believe it can be. It is as simple and as powerful as that. With the new old energy—because truly it is old energy; your scientists are going to tell you that the energy that comes from the central sun started out a long, long time ago before this lifetime, as you understand years and measure lifetimes—you will manifest the shift.

Now it is here, and it will continue to be here for some time yet. So take hold of it. Manifest that which you want to manifest. Become One with your dreams. Do not be afraid to dream. Do not say, "Well, I'm too old. I don't have the golden coins for it. It's probably not going to be accepted by the brothers and sisters. They're going to think it's a crazy idea. I don't think I can do it on my own."

Dream. Dream big, because it is possible. You now have an accentuated energy that is helping you along with whatever has been your dream. If you do not have a clear dream about it, sit and take off all the limitations and say, "How would I like it to be? You know, if I had all of the golden coins that it would take and if I had a group of people, maybe even a small group—it does not have to be a big group—to work with me on this, I'd really love to bring a group of like-minded people together so that they could get excited and then go on to build their dream, even in physical form. I'm going to make that happen. I want to make that dream happen. I *can* make that dream happen." And you *will* make that dream happen.

You are free, you see. Dream big. Do not be afraid to dream. If you feel held back by a partner or so, do what is necessary for the partner. Bring them along with you if you can. If you cannot, do what is necessary for them, but do not let that hold you back. Go for it. You will never ever have a chance as strong as this one. You will never ever, so take hold of the reins and ride the energy.

Dream big. Use the galactic energy that is now coming to you free. There is no charge for it. Nobody in your world has figured out yet how to charge for it. So until they do—and that is doubtful—use it. It is free for the taking.

Your belief system is expanding. It is taking hold of the energy that is streaming into you and you are going with it as far as you want to go with it. Dream big. Do not put boundaries around it. Do not say, "Yes, but...." Say, "Yes; now how do I do it?"

How you do it is by becoming One with it, knowing that you already have it, knowing that perhaps the form of it, the shape of it, how it looks may be a bit different than how you have visualized it; that it will shift and change, but that is good, because it always shifts and changes for the better. A new idea comes in.

Know that truly this is the beginning of the rest of your life. What are you going to do with it?

So be it.

DO YOU KNOW HOW BLESSED YOU ARE?

Beloved one, when you first thought to create, you left a part of you, an awareness of you that is still with you. You turned from it and you said, "I want to create. What can I create?" And you have created all worlds, all scenarios, everything that you can imagine in this lifetime and more because you wanted to know your creative ability.

At first your creations were from Love and from the Isness of Being. Then, later the creative Energy desired to know what else there could be, what could be unlike Love. So you began an experiment. You wanted to know, "How does it feel to be completely immersed in my creation and to be creatively challenged by someone else's creation?"

You went through incarnations where you devised a form, and someone seemingly apart from you devised a creation that came along and destroyed your creation or challenged it in some way. This is happening still, as your news media reports to you, but you have also come to a place where you are ascending.

Now, there has been much talk about ascension, much talk of moving from third dimensional consciousness into fifth dimensional, and truly the numbers do not matter. Ones have said, "Well, what happened to fourth dimension? Did I just go past it in my sleep?" Well, you can say that. Fifth dimension, as you have defined it, is the place where you find yourself ascending into peace with yourself and with other ones and with what is happening in the world.

When you can come to the place where you recognize that everything happens for the grand purpose of awakening and you take the deep breath and abide in peace, you abide in the spirit of yourself; not in the worldly spirit.

As you will practice, as you will repeat being in the space of peace and allowance, looking for the blessing in everything, you will find that it is easier to return to the place of Home and to abide there longer. You are then achieving the ascension.

Now, the ascension which is spoken about and is so highly desired is going to be the ascension of the collective consciousness. It will seem to come about gradually, being done by one person—as you see individuality—and by another person, by another person, according to their own choice and their own soul timetable. Eventually, when there comes the recognition that there is truly only One of us, then the collective consciousness will acknowledge, "I have ascended. I have brought together all of my parts and I have remembered my Oneness." Then the ascension will be known consciously.

You know ascension already. You can feel it, you can imagine it as we speak of it. But to live in that space all of the time is yet a bit of a challenge, as the world will come in and say, "Yes, but how do you feel about surprises? Can you take surprises in stride and see that truly they serve a great purpose?"

Or, as I have seen you have expectations—and expectations are part of the human scene—when those expectations do not manifest exactly, there is then a time of judgment, and you are very quick to judge.

I know that feeling. As a small one, I also had expectations, expectations of what my mother, my father, what society of the village would be doing, and expectations of what *I* should do. But I came to the realization that those expectations were only temporary and passing, and I saw that I could come through the expectations. Perhaps if they were not met in the way that I thought they were going to be met, the way it worked out was better.

So I gave up having expectations. That is difficult in the human realm to do, but you can do it and you can feel the peace that comes with having no expectations as to how things should be or how you should be—or the big one of how "they" should be. That is the one that trips you up most often.

On the other hand, give yourself the gold stars for how soon you give up the expectations when they are not met. Some time ago you would have held onto the disappointment of the expectation not being met. Now you look at it and you have feelings about it, you have judgments about it, and then you say, "Well, there must be more to this than what I see."

You can measure—and give yourself the gold star—as to how speedily you move from the judgment to the place of allowance. I have seen you do this, where you have very, very strong emotion about something, and then after a while you find yourself saying, "Well, that was my expectation based on the information that I had at the time."

As you stand back from it, you can see the bigger picture. As you practice you will find yourself blessed by a gift that you give to yourself, the gift of peace, the gift of allowance, the gift of joy that says, "Hey, this is better than what I thought it was going to be."

Then you have arrived Home—for a moment or so. It does not usually last for a long time, but it lasts long enough that you can measure it, and you can feel happy about yourself and say, "Well, if I did that once, perhaps I can do it again." It becomes easier each time, because you have had the practice and the experience of allowance.

There is a good bit of wisdom that comes with the years if you will allow it, a good bit of wisdom that comes when enough expectations have not been met the way you thought they were going to be met, and you had to deal with something that was actually even better. But sometimes you do not see the better-ness of it until you get into the hindsight and see how it all fits together. That usually takes a bit of time and a bit of wisdom; then you abide in the space of allowance.

You are very blessed by everything that you create, even if it looks like manure in the first place. It allows you to grow. Even if the mate will say to you, "I don't love you anymore. Go find yourself someone else." Even if it looks like there is going to be warring factions of the different geo-political groupings, and perhaps you may be called upon to be part of it, you can step back and see peace instead. Even if the employment says, "It's time for a change. We're changing everything in the structure of this grouping, and we're not going to need you any longer. We're replacing you with some technology. It can think faster; it can compute faster; it can keep better records than you do. Therefore, your position is no longer needed with this company."

Your first feeling is, "Oh, my goodness, what do I do now? I need to be needed, and I need the golden coins because I have promised others that I will pay them the golden coins." So there is a moment or so—usually longer—when you have to get very creative and see, "Okay, where else am I needed?"

Sometimes you have found that the best way to find where you are needed is to volunteer at a place where perhaps the golden coins are not given. You do not need the golden coins quite yet, but you do need to be needed. You do need to serve. So I say to those of you who may be in transition, find a place where you can serve. Later the golden coins will come to you. But you may find that in serving, the exchange of gratitude, the exchange of being needed, the exchange of being worthy—of self-worth—is more valuable than all the golden coins that you used to get from the former employment.

I know that many are going through transitions now where there are changes happening, and I know that many are wondering, "What is the morrow going to bring?" But I say unto you, the morrow is going to bring that which serves you best, even if it does not look like it at first appearance. Later you will be able to look back at it and you will be able to see the blessing in it.

Many times blessings are quite visible. They are right in front of you, such as in the morning when the sun greets you. Maybe it will not stay out all day, but perhaps it will greet you in the morning. Or perhaps you will see it by the end of the day in the sunset, and you will see the beautiful colors that you now have eyes to see.

Know you that a long time ago you did not see all of the colors that you see now? Early in your manifestation the human form was not designed to see various vibrations of color. And in your history—it is even in your science if you can go back and research it far enough back—everything appeared in your creation as black and white and shades of gray. Then part of your creativity was, "How can we change vibration so that we see a little differently?" And you then created eyes that would be receptors of different vibrations.

The same thing occurred with your hearing. At first the hearing was not attuned the way it is now. You went through a period when the hearing was more sensitive than it is now, as you observe even now with your animals. But it was felt to be a big nuisance to have more vibration coming at the ears, and so you toned it down a bit. You have noticed that perhaps as ones gain years and wisdom, sometimes the hearing also changes to the place where ones can listen not so much outwardly but inwardly, although they may not be completely happy about it and they may not see it as a blessing. But it is for a purpose.

In this day and time, there is much that you do not see, and that also is for a purpose: so that you do not get overwhelmed by the vibrations that are all around you. You have the most wonderful technology of your computers that connect you up with brothers and sisters whom you may never see with the physical eyes, but you can connect on the internet and get to know the person by what is written.

The wireless vibrations are right here with you, but you have devised an exclusionary technique so that you are not overwhelmed. In addition, you have quite a few vibrations surrounding you from the brothers and sisters. You are all vibrating with life. You are all putting out your own vibration. The plants are vibrating their life energy. The electric lights are putting out vibration. You are surrounded by vibrations.

As you go within, to the place of peace within, you will find vibration, the vibratory rate of your own in that peace. You can tune-in to it, as you will tune-in to music. It will be your own theme song, and it will feel familiar when you go to the space that is your own. You have felt this when you have been quiet and you have been in meditation. You have felt your own vibration, your own space, and you know it when you are there. You know how to come again to the place which is Home within you, the place of peace which is yours.

As you sit in quietness, you come to a place that truly could be equated to a vibrational musical note. You each have your own note, and when you are there, there is nothing else. When you are in the space that is you, in the tone that is you, there is nothing else for a moment. It is where you live, move, and have your being, right there in that vibration.

Whenever the world comes knocking at your door, you can return quickly to the space which is yours and yours alone. Now, having said "yours and yours alone", is there anyone else who shares that space, that tone with you? If, in Truth, there is only one of us—and I assure you that this is True—yes. But it is just not one single tone. It is a whole broad spectrum of vibration that is shared as the One, as in the rainbow.

You are, in essence, a tone, but as the energy that you have incorporated you have a vibratory rate, and it changes. You can see this when ones do the photograph of the aura. You see the vibratory rate around you and you can see it change even with your thoughts, and the vibration within you changes also.

You are very much in motion all of the time. Even when you feel you are at peace and very quiet, you are still vibrating, because everything is energy. You resonate at a certain frequency, but you do not always stay at that frequency. It changes moment by moment. It changes as you talk with someone. You may find someone and feel, "I really vibrate with her. I'm really in resonance with her. I know this one, and when I'm with her, we're just in tune." Yes, you are. You have met at the same vibratory level, and you feel that with certain people. With other ones, it may take you a while before you reach the place of resonance, but it comes.

You have built into this lifetime, subtle though it may be, opportunity to know your Oneness, to *feel* your Oneness, to allow the body to be in tune with the most beautiful sunsets, as you have devised the colors in this time. You have devised another time when you did not see the various colors. And I say unto you that there is going to come a time when you are going to see other colors that you cannot even dream of right now. You are going to be moving and flowing in a form that you would identify now as liquid crystal, beautiful flowing vibratory liquid—I say liquid because it flows—crystal.

You are going to change the carbon base to a crystalline base. That is already in process. Sometimes there are days when you feel a little bit strange, and that is because things are changing; not outside of you, but within you.

It is a gradual process, although there are ones who want to hurry it up sometimes and they use various substances that put them in an altered state, which can create a bit of confusion. It is their attempt to change that which has been very dense carbon-based to something that flows as the divine spirit that we are.

You are blessed by all of nature that you have put around you. You look unto the mountains from whence cometh your help. Your help cometh from on high (a higher consciousness) and the mountains signify that for you. As you will lift up your eyes to the top of the mountains it allows you to come up higher in your consciousness, recognizing that you can be on top of the mountain and you can be in the valley looking at yourself on top of the mountain and vice versa. You can be on top of the mountain looking at yourself in the valley, and it is all One.

You have the flowing waters, the blessedness of water that lubricates the body and the vibration of the body. You have the flowing waters and the creatures that live within the waters, the fish that swim and jump so beautifully. You have the trees that give you the precious oxygen that you need to breathe. You watch them as they come into flower and into leaf, and you watch them as the colors change and the leaves float softly down. And then you know that in the next season they will be coming back; new leaves, new extension of life. You are surrounded by miracles.

You can love the one who is most difficult to get along with, and in doing so, you recognize a capacity that you did not know you had, a capacity to love that which you do not even like: "But I can love you and allow you. I don't have to like you, and I don't have to be in your presence, but I do wish you well. I do love you."

Then you find that, "Hey, if I can love that person, I must have a greater capacity for love than I ever recognized. Maybe I'm not so constricted after all." And with that comes an awakening where you begin to realize, "You know, if I can do that, maybe others can do that as well. Maybe there ***is*** love in the world," and you know that there is.

When I was nailed to the cross I saw the soldiers, the centurions, doing their jobs. Not all of them wanted to be there. Most of them did not like what was going on, but because of generational teaching, they did what was expected of them. In the depths of their souls, it was not something that they wanted to do: to torture brothers and sisters and to create fear, which they thought then brought them power.

So from the cross I loved them, because I could see that they are love, unrecognized; unrecognized love that they had yet to express. And I will share with you that in later incarnations as they brought forth other lives for themselves, they were able to live out that love and to voice their feelings. In the lifetime when they had certain jobs to do, they did not feel that they were free to speak out or to feel.

You are surrounded by gifts, blessedness that you have provided for yourself. You have said, "I will create." And having created that which is unlike love, and having experienced that which is not so comfortable, you have said, "Now I am going to create that which is loving, that which is exciting, that which allows me to expand and to begin to understand the All that I am." You are creating moment by moment the hologram of your reality, and moment by moment you can change it.

You are so blessed. You are greatly, greatly blessed by all of nature, by all of technology as it is used to allow you to know your possibilities and your probabilities and the realities that you bring forth from that technology. You are blessed by everything that is in your awareness. Make your hologram beautiful. Make your hologram in resonance with your Heart.

Blessed art thou.

So be it.

ENDINGS AND BEGINNINGS

You are now at a time when you are going to bless everything with your Light and with your knowing that everything is changing because you have decreed that you want to know heaven on Earth. You want to know Oneness with the brothers and sisters, and you want for *them* to know Oneness.

Your news media are very, very good at giving you the progress report of how divisive all the brothers and sisters can be with each other. But beyond that, there are many prayers that are being offered up, many prayers that ones are living that seek peace and put out the intention for peace.

So when you listen to your news media, you can say, "Yes, that is the appearance, but I know that there's more than that that is happening. I know that this has divine purpose," because it does, even if it does not appear to have. Your news media love to play up the drama. It is what they receive the golden coins for, and more important to them than the golden coins is the fact that they feel powerful because they are the ones deciding what they are going to put in front of you. So you look at it. You do not deny appearances.

I told this to my disciples when they asked about how to do healing. I said, "First of all, you acknowledge the appearance. Then you look beyond what seemingly is unhealed or unholy and you see the person (or situation) in holiness."

You allow yourself to be aware. Do not go through life with the blinders on and say, "I am only going to look at that which is good, because I'm really not strong enough to look at the rest of it and I don't want that in my world." Well, of course, you do not want that in your world. Do not deny that it is happening, but you do not have to abide with it either.

Allow yourself to choose. You have the power of choice, the power to choose to see peace instead of this; to see purpose even in what appears to be disaster and divisiveness. So do not do as some of your brothers and sisters do, and say, "I am going to shut myself off from the world because I don't want negativity in *my* world. I don't want to experience negativity."

You are very, very strong, and you have it in your power to look at the appearance and then to expand upon that appearance to send your intention of peace and wholeness to whatever is being presented to you.

You no longer need to live in the cave and deny the world. Some of the brothers and sisters remember the lifetimes in the cave and they say, "I don't want to know what's going on. It's too ugly." Well, yes, it does appear that way, but how is it going to change if you do not acknowledge it and then see beyond it? Bring your power to it.

You are going to have the ups and you are going to have the downs; at least that is the way it is going to appear. But the other part of the roller coaster is the fun of it. Why do you go to an amusement park and pay golden coins in order to get onto the roller coaster if it is not for the fun of it? Like, "Wow, oh, my God, oh! But I love it. And I'm going to go back on it again!"

I have heard you and the brothers and sisters say that. "Wow! That was really great. I didn't know if I'd really get through it. I'm going to go back on it again." And, in essence, that is what you do from time to time with the experiences of the world.

This is a good time for finding your center, for finding your peaceful place amidst all of the changes that are happening. Call everything good. Know that everything that is presented to you has a purpose—and the purpose is not to upset you. Now, I know that is the first reaction that oftentimes comes along.

"How could this happen? Why did I bring this to myself?" You brought it because you want to know how strong you are. You want to know how your intention can come to bear upon what seems to be manure, and how you can grow the most lovely garden out of that manure. So count it all as good.

Two thousand years ago there was much of strife, much of divisiveness, much of ones seeking to have power over other ones; similar to today. I came and I spoke the truth of your being, and that truly this was happening, yes; I did not deny appearances. But I said, "You are more than that. You are greatly loved by your Father, Abba—Father/Mother/God/Goddess/All That Is. You are greatly loved and you are always taken care of. You are *always* taken care of. You are always guided and taken care of." Hear that well.

Rest in the knowing that no matter how you see something happening, it is there for a purpose and it is there for a *good* purpose. Look beyond the appearances and trust the strength of yourself within.

Now, you have been practicing coming through all kinds of challenges. You have been bringing up challenges for yourself. You have come through them and you have come to the place where you have said, "Wow! I didn't know I could do that. I thought maybe I had to throw in the towel and be finished. But hey, I'm still here, and I'm even enjoying all of the challenges."

When you get to the point where you can acknowledge the master that you are, when you can come to the place where you look upon all of the choices, all of the challenges and you can be joyful about them and know that truly they are just passing and temporary—which they are—resting in your divine Self, then you recognize and know, truly know, the master that you are.

This is a time of endings—endings of some things that you have thought would be there for much longer, maybe forever—and a time of beginnings, a time when you are going to be finishing old issues; you are going to be completing with things that you have wanted to know intimately and wondering if you *could* know intimately and still survive, and yes, you can, and yes, you will.

It is a time of beginnings as well, because once you come through the challenges that seem to be ending everything that you have trusted and relied upon, you are going to know that you have moved into a new space—sometimes on the physical level, but more than that, on the emotional level.

The emotions are very strong. They do propel you in the choices that you make. Emotions are there to allow you to know the energy that you are. Emotions are energy in motion—e-motion. They can be very, very strong and they can bring up old fears, which is what truly you are asking them to do so that you can look upon those old fears and say, "But that was just the belief that I had. I thought that it had power over me, but I choose anew. I choose to know that everything works for good," and it does.

Everything works together to bring about the realization of Oneness, of the Awakening, as it has been called; awakening to your Oneness and the power of that Oneness. So trust. Trust the endings. Trust the beginnings.

Nothing is ever lost. Everything you have ever experienced in any lifetime is within your soul. The soul is the repository of all of the experiences of all of the lifetimes that you have ever had. And the soul is very, very rich because this is not your first lifetime. You know that. You have remembrances that come to you and you question, "Where did that come from? How do I know certain things before they occur or as they occur?" Because you have already lived those experiences.

This is not your first lifetime, and it is probably not the last incarnation; in fact, it is not your last incarnation. However, the next incarnation may not be on holy Mother Earth. You may choose an incarnation in another dimension, another reality; you will make for yourself another hologram to play with.

It may not be an incarnation with a human form. It may be an incarnation as liquid crystal Light. Anything that you can imagine, you can experience and make manifest. You are very creative, so you will incarnate perhaps with a form or you will come to experience just as the Light and the Beingness that you are.

There is no one who is going to deny you your power to express in *any* form, the same as when you were before *this* incarnation and you looked at what could be and you made choice as to when you would come and what culture you would come into and what your purpose would be.

Now, your universal purpose is to be the creative Energy that you are; that is the bottom line: to express the creative Energy. But how you do that is most wonderful, because it is open, completely open to whatever you want it to be. You made a new beginning when you decided that you would be born into this culture, or if not born into this culture, then to make trek to place yourself later into a certain geographical location.

If you were not born in the same geographical location, there was a knowing that you would come and be with others of like mind, even if it took some searching to find them, but you would find them. And you knew that there would be soul purpose on the individual level, things that you wanted to know intimately and to be complete with, and also on the collective level, that you would work with the collective in order to open some doors and windows for the collective, which you have been doing, because from time to time you have spoken of new ideas.

Maybe ones have accepted those ideas and maybe they have not. Maybe they have said, "There goes that old fool again, thinking such and such. Or there is that young fool who believes that she can…etc." But you have opened some doors and windows, and if ones have not walked through the doors, that is their choice. At least you have pointed out that there is a door and there may be a new way of looking at something.

They might not have even thought of it unless you had said, "Well, you know, this is what I believe. It may seem sort of far out." A lot of the brothers and sisters two thousand years ago thought that what I spoke of was far out, blasphemy. It was not what was taught in the Temple. How could I speak intimately of the Father's love? How could I speak that everyone was loved and that you did not have to kill an animal in order to be holy? Even in this day and time that belief is still held by some: that there must be sacrifice either of an animal or of something dear to you.

So I spoke ideas that were rather radical at that time and are still radical if ones actually understand what I was saying. But it allows you to walk through a door into another reality; maybe a reality that you did not know was there or you have been afraid of walking through. At least you have the knowing that the door is there, and it will keep nagging at you until you do walk through it.

I know your feeling of saying, "Okay, well, maybe tomorrow. I'll play with that idea, but I'm not sure I'm going to actually put it into practice."

You carry fears with you in the knapsack on the back and you say, "Oh, this is so heavy. I don't know if I can keep on carrying this." And then when you get the courage to say, "Okay, let's get the knapsack out here and look at what's in it," it is seen to be a no-thing, a nothing, and it disappears. It dissolves into the nothingness that it has always been.

But until you get to that point, it is a really a big fear and it is heavy, and you carry it from lifetime to lifetime until finally you say, "Enough already. I'm going to look at it. And maybe it is hell itself. I've been told that that's a really bad place to go." And then you open up the knapsack and you take out what has been termed "hell" and you find out that it is nothing more than a belief, something that has been taught to you from someone else, passed down generation to generation.

The only hell is the hell that you make for yourself in the present moment of fearing something, and oftentimes you have lived with that hell a whole lifetime. Then there has come a lifetime where you have said or someone has said to you, "Hey, you know, let's look at this idea." And you bring it out into the open. "Let's look at this fear. What is it that you really, really feel that's making the body tremble?"

You know that feeling, where the body just collapses in on itself and you feel so sick. Then you get to the heart of the matter and you say, "This does not have power over me. I'm the one creating it; therefore, I'm going to un-create it." You look at it and you can look right through it. But until you get to that place, it is agony.

You know what I am speaking of. It may come to you in the middle of the night, and it will feel even darker in the middle of the night. But as you breathe, as you trust, as you call out to your angels, guides, teachers—and we are always around you—we will be with you. We cannot be anywhere else, truly, since there is no separation, and you are the Light, the same as we are, except that you put on the sunshades and everything seems to be dark.

In the darkest moments we are with you. In your lightest moments we are with you. When you decease the body, which is a great fear because the body says to you that it wants to keep on keeping on and so there is great fear... but when you decease the body, you go to your own Light. There is a brilliance of Light. Even your researchers have spoken of this.

There is energy that has been measured from the living body, and then it has been compared to the weight of the body which has allowed the soul to leave it. It can be weighed and measured. The Light that you go to is so brilliant that you will think that someone must have turned on a billion light bulbs. And all of the ones you have ever loved are there. If they have laid down the body, they are there to welcome you, and there is great joy and rejoicing and great love. It is Home.

It is what you are seeking even as you are incarnate. You are seeking the new beginning of knowing Home and love that is unlimited. So do not fear releasing the body. Now, I am not saying to you that you need to rush forward into deceasing the body, but allow yourself to be at peace, knowing that truly you are going to live your purpose.

And when your purpose has been fulfilled, there is going to be great rejoicing, a brilliance of Light—as we have said many times—brought about by a great miracle that you have contained it in the physicality, and when you are finished with the physicality and you are ending that part of your experience and beginning a new beginning, you will see your own Light and it will be overwhelming in its Love.

So I want you to take this with you in this time: how loved you are and how you are surrounded by Love. Even though you do not see the loved ones who have gone on before, they are with you. Some of you are open to knowing the presence of loved ones around you, because they *are* around you all the time, speaking to you, bringing you up, if you will let them, to a place where there is only love and encouragement, allowing you to know the greatness of the Light that you are and the miracle of choosing to live a hologram that says that there can be other than Light, other than joy and rejoicing.

And when you have fulfilled your purpose—to live from the place of love in every encounter, to trust that love and to know that as it comes forth from you it has to flow through you and you are blessed—there remains only Love and Light.

Every day, every moment of every day is a celebration of life if you will see it thus. Yes, I know that there are messages of the world, messages of the mind that sometimes question, but at the heart of everything is the Truth that you are *always* taken care of and that you are *always* in Love. It cannot be otherwise.

So even when the darkest of dark comes knocking at your door in the middle of the night, allow yourself, if you want to, to get up and to switch on the light on the desk or the overhead light and to say, "Nothing can penetrate the Light that I am—which is true—I go forward in that Light, trusting that always I am guided, loved, and taken care of. What is there to fear?"

One of your wise men has said, "There is nothing to fear except fear itself." I know that it can be very strong and put a stranglehold on you for a moment or so, but it is not real. Only Love is Real—capital "R"—only Love, and how loved you are.

So if something comes to you in the middle of the night and it feels like the end of everything, get up, put on the light, put on your own Light, turn it on, and know that truly it is the beginning of your Awakening. And know that I meet you in Light.

Every ending is a beginning. Every ending of a fear is a beginning of new life, new awareness. Rejoice in every ending, because it is a beginning. You are going beyond and leaving behind that which was and does not serve you any longer.

Rejoice, beloved one. Live in joy. Live in Love and know that you are well and truly loved.

So be it.

ABSOLUTE LOVE, INFINITE LIGHT

Now, beloved one, we are going to talk about a vast subject. We are going to talk about God.

First of all, God is not an entity. It is not a He. It is not a She. It is not even an It. God is beyond description, yet the human mind wants to know and wants to define and redefine and change. And that is good, because every time you change, you allow an expansion of the consciousness to take in more.

You are God, an essence of God, right here, expressing. You are going to say, "Well, that must be a very tiny percentage of God." It depends on your self-image, does it not? I will say that you are *all* of God right here. You do not always activate it. You do not always tune in to it, all of it, but you are God having an experience as a human.

This is not the first experience you have ever had. You keep adding to it, which is one of the most beautiful things about God. God cannot be contained, cannot be defined in any human terms, any human verbiage. It is beyond all of that, and yet you are the essence come once again to play, come once again to create, come once again to assume a definition, and yet in assuming a definition, you are already limiting God.

I have spoken often that God is Love, and have said to you that love is the closest thing in your experience to understanding the expansiveness of God. When you fall in love with someone, you forget small self. You want to know where they are, what they are doing, what they are thinking, and you cannot wait to meet up with them one more time and to ask, "What have you done in this day? Who did you speak with? What are the ideas that you had today?" You forget yourself, the small self, in love with another one.

I have to use human words to explain God, but God cannot be known by the mind. It cannot be known by definition. It cannot be known by words. But words can be clues as to a feeling, the feeling of expansiveness, the feeling of Allness, the feeling of being accepted without even having to think about being accepted. There is not a thought.

In the love of God, there is not thought. It is an Is-ness of feeling of being beyond anything that you know in human terms. But human love can give you a clue. Therefore, you have put together the molecules of our holy Mother, the Earth, the dust of the Earth, to make a body. You have brought together energy in a form to express that love, to be able to speak, to hold, to gaze into another's eyes, and to lose yourself in another's eyes; being able to forget small self.

This does not have to be just with another human person. It can be with a beloved pet. You look into their eyes and you lose yourself momentarily or longer. You lose yourself in the love with them. And you think, even with a thought which is not a thought, "I am One with this that I love. I am One with this person", or "I am One with the pet. I am One in love with anyone and everyone."

You come to a place, as your great masters have, where all they live in is love. They do not judge. It is love without judgment. It is love without mind. It is love without thought. It does not judge, because there is nothing to judge. Everything Is, and everything is non-judged. It is Love.

You know, when you are in love with someone, you do not judge. You abide in the place of non-judgment of them, the same as you are hoping that they will not be judging you.

For truly, if they are in love with you, they do not judge. There is not thought. There is only the feeling of Allness, the feeling that, "I have come Home." Sometimes you find it with another person. Sometimes you find it even in a sentence in a book, where the lights go on and you know that you are Home in that moment. Or someone may say something to you and all of a sudden you are accepted in that feeling, and you know that you are Home.

It is a most wonderful true place to be. For truly what you are searching for is to know the feeling of acceptance, the feeling of non-judgment, the feeling of love, where you know that you are perfect. Now, your world does not tell you that. Your world says that always you must be striving to make yourself better. From the time that you were the small infant, the parents have said to you that you are not quite perfect. You could be better. And by several different means, they try to impress upon you that you could be better.

Even if you come home from your schooling and you have brought the top marks, the parents, in their desire to make you better, will say, "Well, now, make sure you do this again next month." And so you say, "But I thought I had already reached that place," and yes, you have. But it is the parents' way of wanting to see you perfect, and you are already perfect.

It is the parents' misguided love—I will put it that way—where they feel they should be able to guide you, mold you, shape you according to their idea of perfection. But it must be left open-ended for you to live out your own perfection, which you may acknowledge later, unless you go into a repetition with the one that you are partners with who is then exampling for you what the parents were doing, and you might live that for a time, or maybe two or three times or more, until finally you have an incarnation where you know—you bring enough remembrance with you from the space of God—where you know that you are perfect already.

You have met ones who seem to go bouncing along through life as the most wonderful beings, and you wonder, "What secret do they know?" They know their perfection. They know that they have come here perfect. But they are yet few in number, because your world is a very strong and harsh taskmaster.

Your world is full of "shoulds", as you know. My world two thousand years ago had "shoulds" in it as well. There were times when I needed to sit by flowing water and watch the water, which did not judge itself. It only exampled that which it is: the molecules of energy in the shape of water forever flowing. And I understood from that that I was energy also, that I had made myself in a certain form and fashion, but truly I was the Father's work.

And I spoke to you of the loving Father which is beyond the human father, because human fathers can sometimes miss the mark a little bit or quite a bit. So, I hope you understand that the Father that I speak of, Abba, is forever loving, because you are Love Itself incarnate, walking around, creating, experiencing.

It behooves you, if you are Love—and I assure you that you are—to be loving; to be loving to the other ones that you have interaction with, but even more than that, to be loving to self. If you do not love self, who *is* going to love you?

When you take time for self in meditation and quiet, and you commune with the Allness that you are, with the peace that you are, you are touching and living in and dwelling in the Love of God, the Allness of absolute Love that knows no other, knows no judgment, knows no thought, knows only Is-ness of peace, absolute Love; nothing else exists.

The world is going to say, "Well, those are nice words, but what about the things that I have agreed that I will do? What about the decisions that I have to make? People are waiting for me to make a decision." I assure you that as you will spend a bit of time for yourself in peace and in quiet, the answers will come to you without having to run around in a frenzy trying to decide what is right. You will know. There will be a quiet knowing that comes to you.

Allow yourself to abide in peace, because that is your birthright. That is from whence you have come, and it is where you are going to go after you lay down the body and have no further use for it. You are going to go to perfect peace.

Now, I know you have stories. Your religious/philosophical organizations and your authorities, who seem to know more, have given you many stories of what happens after you lay down the body. But, fortunately, some clues have come to you that suggest that you go to a Light; that there is a Light at the end of the tunnel, and you go to that Light.

That Light is your own. That Light is the Light that you are, even while you are focusing upon a human incarnation. You *are* infinite Light, and you have come from a place of Light. You have come from a consciousness of knowing Light. "And in Him there is no darkness." Now, I would change that quotation to say, "In God—it is not a gender—there is no darkness. There is only Light."

You are Light right now as you are activating the body. Your scientists are proving that to you when you have the aura photographs taken and you see the Light around you. Where is that Light coming from? It is coming from you. That is why it changes from time to time, depending on your emotions (energy in motion) and consciousness. You may have a photograph done one day, and you come back the next day and have the photograph taken, and the Light will be different.

The next time you have opportunity to have the aura photographed, allow yourself to be very, very joyous, because when you are happy—like the little child who rejoices in life— at that point the aura stretches very large.

You *are* infinite Light. You have come from infinite Light, and infinite Light you will return to when you are finished with the capsule that you have made for yourself to walk around with. When you are finished with this reality, then you will return to the Light, the Light that you are.

You have the most wonderful clues coming for you now, where you do not have to believe that you are going to spend a certain number of years in a place that is going to cleanse you of all of your sins, or in a place that is going to cleanse you by the burning. You know, I have always wondered about that, in that if you burn something, what does it turn into? Ash. And is that clean? You would most often say that ashes are a bit on the dirty side, a bit that you want to wash off. So I have always wondered about that one, how the fire is going to cleanse you. Okay, that is a rumor. That is a story. You have it on good authority that it is not true.

That idea has been given to you to keep you in shape, in form, and to follow "the ones who must know better than I do. What they tell me must be true. I'm not quite sure why, but I've been told that they know better than I do." So your authorities, your pseudo masters have given you all kinds of stories to keep you in line, to make you follow whatever they wanted you to follow, and—the bottom line—to give your golden coins to the preservation of that story.

The golden coins always seem to be the bottom line—in this world anyway. There is nothing wrong with golden coins. However, if the ownership of golden coins has you owned, then that is where the problem would be. But there is nothing wrong with golden coins, even many golden coins.

You have examples of ones who have many of the golden coins, and they do much good with allowing others to benefit from their giving and their vision of sharing. Some of the other ones, because of past lifetimes where they felt that they did not have enough of the golden coins, will try to keep them as long as they can.

But then, as you have understood from your own lifetimes, the golden coins cannot bring you security, happiness, good health. It is a false belief and a false god to be worshipped. You have, for the most part, come to a balance of understanding golden coins. They are to be used to further the ideals of love and compassion, of Oneness.

Now, as you have seen, in order to define God, you have clues. But any definition you come up with is not the Allness of God, for God cannot be defined or limited. God does not fit into a small package. God is *this* and more. So when we speak that God is Love, that is a clue to the feeling of God, the feeling of expansiveness, the feeling of peace and the feeling of total acceptance.

For God, if it were a person, would look upon you and see no fault. And God is more than that. It is, as I have said, absolute Love that knows nothing different than Love. And you, as the extension of God come into an incarnation, you are the Light, the Energy of Love. You have put God Energy into manifest form of Light energy, and you have taken a quality from the Allness to demonstrate, to know for yourself that you are much more than just the little speck of dust that some of your religious/philosophical leaders have *said* that you are—only a little speck of dust.

You are much more than that. You contain within the consciousness, as you allow it to accept and to bring in the Allness, you contain the Allness of God, and yes, you can know it even while being in an incarnation. You have masters who have attained that consciousness, and in seeking the consciousness of Allness it does not mean that there is a denigration of incarnation.

It does not mean that there is anything wrong with choosing an incarnation. In fact, your greatest masters have often chosen an incarnation which is most difficult and requires the most Love.

You can touch the space of Love and Allness. It will change your whole outlook on everything. It will afford you a wider vista of what human life is all about and what Life with a capital "L" is. You are absolute Love which has chosen one more time to bring Itself into a smaller form.

You are infinite Light which has made manifest in the physical the Allness of Love. And you *are* the Light and the Love of Christ. You do not always recognize it in yourself. You sometimes do recognize it in other ones. You can see it in other ones. And in order for you to see it in another one, you have to have a point of reference within yourself; otherwise, you would not see it.

You are the Christ. You *are* the Allness of God come into this area of incarnation, bringing the Allness into a space which can then relate to other ones, because you have said, "I want to know all of my parts." So I say to you, look around. These are all of your parts—and even more.

Go always as the Christ that you are. Christ did not live just two thousand years ago. It was not only embodied in one Yeshua. It lives and moves even in this day and time, and it loves. Allow yourself to live in Love. You are the Absolute Love, the Infinite Light of God.

So be it.

Other books in *Jeshua, The Personal Christ* Series:

Volume I	$12.95
Volume II	$12.95
Volume III: Don't Look For Me in a Tortilla Chip	$12.95
Volume IV: The Interdimensional Self : The Way to Peace	$12.95
Volume V: You Are the Power of the Future	$14.95
Volume VI: You Are the Power of Now	$14.95

Order from Oakbridge University Press

www.oakbridge.org

More books from Oakbridge University Press:

Jesus and Mastership: The Gospel According to Jesus of Nazareth, as Scribed by James Coyle Morgan

Books may be ordered in paperback form by contacting Oakbridge University Press at:

(360) 681-5233
www.oakbridge.org